THE Sunset GRILL

125 Tasty Recipes for Casual Get-Togethers and Easy Weeknight Cookouts

RECIPES BY THE EDITORS OF
Sunset Magazine

FOREWORD BY
Cheryl and Bill Jamison

SUNSET BOOKS
Menlo Park, California

contents

foreword

In our 25 years as food and travel writers, one of our most amazing discoveries occurred by chance in the Schlesinger Library of Radcliffe Institute on the campus of Harvard University. Browsing the books about barbecuing and grilling, we came across an extraordinary, wood-bound volume from 1938 that heralded a new era in American outdoor cooking.

It was *Sunset's Barbecue Book*. Written before manufactured metal grills became widely available, the book showed readers how to construct a brick or stone fireplace or pit in their backyards for cooking, and explained why it would make an inviting focal point for outdoor living and entertaining.

The *Sunset* editors were way ahead of the curve on the notion of outdoor kitchens, which has become a major trend nationwide in just the last dozen years. They also provided the earliest tips we've ever found for successful patio parties, and presented some of the first American recipes for backyard dishes. The pioneering book established *Sunset* as a bold and imaginative publisher in the field, and it has remained in the forefront ever since, releasing new and updated cookbooks on a regular basis.

In writing our own dozen cookbooks, we've found frequent inspiration in *Sunset* publications, including our monthly copies of the magazine itself, which we started subscribing to shortly after we moved to the Rocky Mountain West three decades ago. In our early years in the region, wanting to learn more about Southwestern versions of Mexican dishes, we turned to a *Sunset* cookbook. Friends and neighbors often look in the same direction for help. At numerous dinner parties over time when we've complimented a dish, the host or hostess has proudly confided to us, "It's a *Sunset* recipe."

We know from long experience that *Sunset* recipes work. Authoritative yet accessible to any home cook, they always offer a tested sense of reliability and can also be counted on to bring a dash of sophistication to family meals and casual entertaining. The flavor of many of the dishes reflects a Western sense of place, but always in a welcoming way that cheers fans in all areas of the country.

America's backyard grilling revolution and its natural companion, easy entertaining, grew up together—initially in the West, nurtured by *Sunset*'s devoted enthusiasm. In a time now when cooks everywhere embrace the passion, the editors of *The Sunset Grill* continue to stoke the outdoor fires on behalf of us all. We're confident that readers will gain as much from this latest collection of recipes as we and others have from previous publications. It's even possible that you will be as tickled with this book as we were at the Schlesinger Library with the 1938 original, 70 years young this year.

—Cheryl and Bill Jamison

the sunset grill

Here at *Sunset,* we believe grilling is the ultimate modern cooking method. Casual, low fuss, and fun, it's a great way to enjoy meals with family and friends—whether you are getting dinner on the table on a busy weeknight or relaxing in the backyard on a Saturday afternoon. A style we call *The Sunset Grill.*

Casual Get-Togethers

Gathering around the grill in the backyard is the perfect way to entertain with ease. The grill itself is an instant icebreaker, and conversation flows easily over an informal meal. A little planning and prep means that food is ready to cook and serve quickly when guests arrive, but impromptu dinners can be as simple as lighting the fire and setting the backyard table. Delicious dishes like Tri-Tip with Shiraz and Soy (page 192) or Wine-Brined Grilled Chicken (page 132) are easy to prepare and sophisticated enough to anchor any party. To pull together the perfect weekend evening, just add a few easy nibbles, full-flavored side dishes, a bottle of wine, and plenty of good friends.

Easy Weeknight Meals

During busy, pressured weeks, it can be tough to get a good family meal on the table quickly and easily. Grilling is the ideal solution: You can often marinate meat or poultry ahead of time, toss the main course and sides on the grill for quick cooking, and then clean up in a flash. Weeknight dinners on the grill can be as simple or as fancy as you like. Look to dishes like Grilled Chicken with Lime and Pepper (page 116) or Shrimp Satay (page 95) for fast dinners that help keep the family meal fun for both cook and diners.

The Art of Backyard Dining

The beauty of backyard dining is that it's instantly relaxed. Just think of your yard or patio as an extension of your home. Depending on the occasion, you can dress the table up or down with linens, plates, and easy flower arrangements. And let the great outdoors, and great food and drink, do the rest!

Ideas for Relaxed Entertaining

You don't need to go to a lot of trouble to make your table shine. All it takes is one creative idea or special touch, placed so that it will catch a diner's eye. Simple table decorations and serving presentations complement the laid-back feel of alfresco dining.

SET THE SCENE—Alternate miniature lanterns and flowers in a row down the center of the table for a summery look. Pull it together by coordinating the flowers with the colors of the linen.

KEEP IT SIMPLE—Skip elaborate plating outdoors. Instead, present a casual arrangement of tempting appetizers like herb-skewered Spiedini di Mozzarella (page 36) on a simple board, and guests can nibble with ease.

TAKE A SIP—Don't fuss over wine service. Offer refreshing wines like dry rosés or light whites in small, narrow glasses, and let guests help themselves to an aperitif.

PLAN AHEAD—Look for recipes that offer the option to prepare ahead. You can marinate Brick-Grilled Cornish Hens (page 136), and other recipes like it, overnight in the refrigerator.

WRAP IT UP—Roll flatware in crisp sheets of parchment paper or vellum for guests to grab. Add a pretty detail by tucking a cheery gerbera daisy in each packet.

WHET THE APPETITE—Set out several tiny bowls of olives or other salty nibbles on tables around the yard to greet guests. A few snacks will make them feel instantly welcome and tease taste buds for the main course.

the easiest party ever

Grilling means easy entertaining, as at this south-of-the-border feast. Planning and cooking ahead are key: Everything in this menu can be prepared in advance. For a relaxed party, transform your backyard into a party space with a few themed touches. Our delicious, easy, no-utensils-required menu keeps prep time and cleanup to a minimum.

Cinco de Mayo, Easy as 1–2–3

Looking for a fun way to kick off the summer grilling season? Cinco de Mayo—a celebration of Mexican liberation that is now celebrated north and south of the border—is timed just right, and its festive, carefree spirit translates perfectly to any gathering around the grill. A make-ahead menu of easy, hearty finger foods with Mexican flavors is perfect for the fifth of May or for any other grilling party. Gather your friends outdoors, offer napkins rather than plates for easy-to-eat fare like Flank Steak Tortitas (page 175) and Garlic Butterflied Shrimp (page 92), and get ready to enjoy your own celebration.

1. COOK BEFORE THE GUESTS ARRIVE

Grilled foods like flank steak and shrimp are just as tasty at room temperature as they are hot. The dips and desserts for this party are easily made ahead.

2. HAVE GUESTS SERVE THEMSELVES

Dips, little sandwiches, and cookies lend themselves to a no-fuss buffet. Arrange foods attractively and let everyone dig in.

3. MINGLE AND ENJOY!

At this relaxed party, guests and host can circulate as they eat and chat. Encourage mixing with informal groupings of tables and chairs.

Setting the Scene

To lend the festivities extra flair, present colorful Mexican sodas—and cervezas, of course—on ice. Look for punched-tin luminarias in Latino markets, or make your own candlelit lanterns with sand-weighted paper bags. Hanging votive jars, suspended with bent wire, also add atmospheric glow. Bright striped linens and chunky earthenware serving plates complete the look.

wine for the grill

Beer with a barbecue is a good choice, but wine adds something extra to even the most casual gathering and is unmatched for food friendliness. Generally speaking, the heartier the fare, the heartier the wine. Move from reds to dry rosés or whites for lighter dishes, or choose a dry sparkling wine to pair with just about any dish. Here are a few more pairing suggestions.

Red

Robust reds tend to be smash hits with hearty grilled meats and other bold-tasting foods from the grill. The concentrated flavors of spicy, jammy Syrah (Shiraz in Australia) and big, rustic Petite Sirah work beautifully with grilled meats. With their fruity aromas and earthy flavors, Old World reds like Spanish Riojas or Rhône varietals from the south of France match happily with grilled lamb or other meats. Zinfandels, with their distinctive berry notes, and Cabernet Sauvignon can be good choices, too. Lighter reds like Old and New World Pinot Noirs complement grilled salmon, duck, or flavorful grilled chicken.

Rosé

Dry rosés, which have grown in popularity of late, are juicy but not heavy—a refreshing summer quaffing wine, and an excellent match for grilled fare from sausages to salmon. Traditional rosés from southern France and Spain, based on such varietals as Grenache, Syrah, or Tempranillo, balance fresh berry flavors with crisp acidity and some mineral notes. In the New World, rosés may be made from almost any red varietal, from Pinot Noir to Sangiovese. Rosés with a hint of sweetness work well with spicy marinades and smoky flavors, but avoid cloying blush wines such as white Zinfandel.

White

Cool whites—from floral to fruity to minerally—match a range of grilled fare. Aromatic, light whites like Riesling and Chenin Blanc pair with lighter grilled chicken, fish, or shrimp. Gewürztraminers or Rieslings with a touch of sweetness complement Asian or spicy flavors. Try crisp Sauvignon Blanc with grilled vegetables or very light grilled fish. The tropical-fruit notes of New Zealand Sauvignon Blancs can be nice with fruity marinades and salsas. Big, oaky flavors may clash with smoke from the grill, so if you're a Chardonnay lover, try unoaked Chardonnays, such as French Chablis or examples being made by a few New World vintners.

Sparkling

Bubbly at a barbecue? Why not? Many enthusiasts believe dry sparkling wine goes well with everything. Plus, it's a refreshing choice on a warm evening, and it takes a party from simple to special in the time it takes to pop the cork. To complement bold flavors from the grill, look for slightly fruity but still dry sparklers like *blancs de noirs* (made from Pinot Noir) or rosé Champagnes or New World pink sparkling wines. A fun, distinctive choice that's becoming easier to find—and that's delicious with everything from hot dogs to ribs—is a red bubbly, such as Australia's sparkling Shiraz.

grill savvy

Cooking over an open flame is elemental. All you need to turn out delicious casual fare every time is a grill, some fuel and basic tools, and a little know-how. With *Sunset's* long history at the grill, we've honed our barbecue method to produce reliably great results. Here's what you need to know.

Fuel for the Fire

With charcoal grills, you have a choice of materials to burn. Most common are manufactured briquets, pressed lumps of charred wood chips. Natural hardwood charcoal, made from pieces of wood, is pricier but burns hotter and imparts a pleasant smoky flavor to food. Hardwood logs, allowed to burn down to embers, are unsuitable for smaller grills but work well in outdoor fireplaces.

Fire Starters

Starting a gas grill is as easy as flipping a switch, and lighting coals can be nearly as simple. Our favorite tool is the inexpensive chimney: Fill its cylinder with crumpled newspaper, lay the briquets on top, and ignite the paper. Plug-in electric starters, buried in a mound of briquets, also get flames going quickly. Avoid resorting to lighter fluid, which imparts an unpleasant taste to food.

Basic Tools

Grilling calls for a few must-have tools: Metal tongs, for turning meat without piercing it, are indispensable, as are metal spatulas and a grill basket for flipping fish. An instant-read thermometer is handy for checking doneness, and a wire brush for cleaning the grill is essential. A long-handled brush lets you paint on sauces during cooking.

Direct Heat

Grilling right over a bed of hot coals or open flame—referred to as the direct-heat method—is perfect for many vegetables and thinner cuts of meat, such as chops, steaks, burgers, sausages, chicken, kebabs, or firm-fleshed fish. Direct-heat grilling is used throughout this book, in recipes like Tenderloin Steaks with Gorgonzola Butter (page 187), Mediterranean Lamb Burgers (page 204), and Grilled Salmon with Blackberry-Cabernet Coulis (page 83). Tender cuts like these can take the heat and will cook through before they burn. Trim meat and poultry well, as excess fat or skin can lead to flare-ups (keep a spray bottle of water on hand to douse any flames). Gas and charcoal grills are equally well suited to direct-heat grilling, but the technique for setting up each type differs.

CHARCOAL—To grill directly over charcoal, plan on lighting the fire about 30 minutes before you want to start cooking. Open your barbecue's dampers, ignite a large mound of charcoal (65 to 75 briquets, or enough to cover the grate in a solid layer) on the firegrate, and let burn until spotted with gray ash, 15 to 25 minutes. Spread the briquets into a solid layer, replace the grill, and let coals burn until they reach the desired temperature. If the fire gets too cool, add a few more coals.

GAS—Direct-heat grilling with a gas grill couldn't be easier. Start by ensuring that your grill is clean, and then ignite the burners and set to high heat. Close the lid of the grill and allow it to preheat for 10 minutes. Then, adjust the burners to your desired temperature, check the grill temperature using the hand test (see "How Hot Is Hot?", at left), and start cooking. Generally, you need to close the grill lid during cooking on a gas grill.

How Hot Is Hot?

Testing grill temperature is easy: Just hold your hand an inch or two above the grate and count the seconds ("one-Mississippi, two-Mississippi ... ") before you need to snatch your hand away. The timing at a glance:

- High heat: 2 to 3 seconds
- Medium-high heat: 3 to 4 seconds
- Medium heat: 4 to 5 seconds

Indirect Heat

Long-cooked foods, delicate items prone to burning, and large cuts of meat can all benefit from the cooler temperature and less intense fire of indirect-heat grilling. Such recipes as Spiced Pulled-Pork Sandwiches (page 163), and Beef Rib Roast with Yorkshire Pudding (page 200) use indirect heat to develop rich long-cooked flavor. In this method, the grill is heated in one area, and the food then cooks over the cooler area rather than over the flame. Charcoal and gas grills are set up for indirect-heat cooking using different methods, though the basic principle remains the same. Whether using charcoal or gas, you'll need to place a disposable drip pan under the food, to protect the inside of the grill from messy drippings.

CHARCOAL—To grill with charcoal over indirect heat, mound 50 to 60 briquets on the firegrate (or use a chimney) and let burn until covered with gray ash, 20 to 30 minutes. Push the hot coals to one side or around the perimeter of the grate, place a disposable drip pan on the side without the coals or within the perimeter, and set the oiled grill rack in place. Grill foods according to recipe instructions, placing them in the indirect-heat area over the drip pan, not over the coals.

GAS—To prepare a gas grill for indirect-heat cooking, turn all burners to high and close the lid. Let preheat for about 10 minutes, or until the temperature inside the grill reaches 350° to 400°F. Lift the lid, turn off one of the burners, and lower the other burner(s) to medium. Place a drip pan under the turned-off burner—this is the indirect-heat area. Set the oiled grill rack in place and cook foods over the indirect-heat area, according to recipe instructions.

Wood Chips Add Flavor

The long, slow smoking of a true barbecue imparts unparalleled flavor to food, but you can get some of the same savor with a simple gas or charcoal grill. To add a delicious smoky taste to foods grilled over direct or indirect heat, soak mesquite or fruitwood chips in water for 30 minutes, then add them to the fire as each recipe directs.

marinades, rubs & salsas

Lemon-Pepper Marinade for Fish and Poultry

1 teaspoon grated lemon zest

1/4 cup fresh lemon juice

2 tablespoons white wine vinegar

2 tablespoons Asian fish sauce (*nuoc mam or nam pla*) or soy sauce

2 tablespoons minced green onion

1 tablespoon sugar

1 tablespoon olive oil

1 teaspoon minced garlic

1/2 teaspoon coarsely ground black pepper

In a small container, mix the lemon zest, lemon juice, vinegar, fish sauce, green onion, sugar, olive oil, garlic, and pepper. Use or cover and chill up to 1 week.

Makes about 1/2 cup

Spiced Cider and Maple Marinade for Poultry and Pork

1/3 cup cider vinegar

2 tablespoons maple syrup

2 tablespoons chopped fresh ginger

1 tablespoon Worcestershire sauce

1 tablespoon olive oil

1 teaspoon fennel seeds

1/4 teaspoon ground allspice

In a blender, mix the vinegar, maple syrup, ginger, Worcestershire sauce, oil, and spices until ginger is finely ground. Use or cover and chill up to 1 week.

Makes about 2/3 cup

Wine and Herb Marinade for Fish, Poultry, and Meat

1/3 cup dry white or red wine

3 tablespoons white or red wine vinegar

2 tablespoons minced shallots

1 tablespoon olive oil

1 tablespoon sugar

1 tablespoon minced garlic

1 tablespoon dry mustard

1 teaspoon *each* dried oregano, dried basil, and dried marjoram

3/4 teaspoon salt

1/4 teaspoon freshly ground black pepper

In a small container, mix the wine (for fish, poultry, or pork, use white wine and white wine vinegar; for beef or lamb, use red), vinegar, shallots, olive oil, sugar, garlic, mustard, dried herbs, salt, and pepper. Use or cover and chill up to 1 week.

Makes about 2/3 cup

Soy-Balsamic Marinade for Fish, Poultry, and Beef

1/4 cup soy sauce

3 tablespoons balsamic vinegar

1 tablespoon honey

1 tablespoon Asian (toasted) sesame oil

1/4 to 1/2 teaspoon red pepper flakes

1 clove garlic, minced

In a small container, mix the soy sauce, vinegar, honey, sesame oil, red pepper flakes, and garlic. Use or cover and chill up to 1 week.

Makes about 1/2 cup

Spice Rub for Fish and Poultry

1/2 teaspoon ground coriander

1/2 teaspoon ground cumin

1/2 teaspoon curry powder

1/4 teaspoon ground ginger

1/4 teaspoon salt

1/8 teaspoon cayenne

In a small bowl, mix the coriander, cumin, curry powder, ginger, salt, and cayenne. Use or keep up to 1 week, stored airtight at room temperature.

Makes about 2 tablespoons

Chipotle-Pepper Rub for Pork and Beef

3 dried chipotle chiles (each about 2 inches long)

2 tablespoons black peppercorns

1 tablespoon pink peppercorns

1 tablespoon coarse salt, such as sea salt or kosher salt

1 tablespoon cumin seed

Heat the chipotles in a microwave oven at full power until they puff up and smell slightly toasted, 15 to 30 seconds. Trim and discard the stems. Slit the chiles open and discard the seeds and veins. Coarsely chop the chiles. In a food processor or spice grinder, pulse the chiles, black peppercorns, pink peppercorns, salt, and cumin seed until finely ground. Use or keep up to 1 week, stored airtight at room temperature.

Makes about 1/3 cup

Herb Spice Rub for Pork and Beef

1/3 cup paprika

2 teaspoons garlic powder

2 teaspoons onion powder

11/2 teaspoons salt

1 teaspoon dry mustard

1 teaspoon ground coriander

1 teaspoon ground or rubbed sage

1 teaspoon dried marjoram

1 teaspoon dried thyme

1 teaspoon freshly ground black pepper

In a bowl, mix the paprika, garlic powder, onion powder, salt, mustard, coriander, sage, marjoram, thyme, and pepper. Use or keep up to 1 week, stored airtight at room temperature.

Makes about 1/2 cup

Spiced Salt Rub for Lamb

3 tablespoons coriander seeds

2 tablespoons fennel seeds

2 tablespoons fine sea salt

1 tablespoon dried thyme

1/2 tablespoon coarsely ground black pepper

In a blender, combine the coriander and fennel seeds and process until finely ground. Add the sea salt, thyme, and pepper and process to combine. Use or keep up to 1 week, stored airtight at room temperature.

Makes about 1/2 cup

Black Bean–Mango Salsa for Fish

1 can (15 ounces) black beans, rinsed and drained

1 cup diced firm-ripe mango

1 large Roma tomato, cored and coarsely chopped

1/2 cup diced orange bell pepper

1/2 cup diced yellow bell pepper

1/4 cup finely diced onion

1 tablespoon minced fresh jalapeño chile

1 tablespoon chopped fresh cilantro

1 clove garlic, minced

2 tablespoons fresh lime juice

1 tablespoon red wine vinegar

Salt and freshly ground black pepper

In a bowl, mix the beans, mango, tomato, bell peppers, onion, jalapeño chile, cilantro, garlic, lime juice, and vinegar. Add salt and pepper to taste. Serve or cover and chill up to 1 day.

Makes about 4 cups

Salsa Cruda for Fish and Poultry

3 fresh Anaheim chiles (9 ounces total)

1 1/2 pounds firm-ripe tomatoes, cored and chopped

2 green onions, ends trimmed, thinly sliced

2 cloves garlic, minced

2 tablespoons chopped fresh cilantro

1 to 3 tablespoons minced fresh serrano chiles (optional)

Salt and freshly ground black pepper

Rinse, stem, seed, and chop the Anaheim chiles. In a bowl, mix the Anaheim chiles, tomatoes, onions, garlic, cilantro, and serrano chiles with salt and pepper to taste. Serve or cover and chill up to 1 day.

Makes about 4 cups

Salsa Chilpequín for Pork and Beef

1/2 cup (about 1 ounce) dried chilpequín or dried chiltepín chiles

2 teaspoons olive oil

2 cloves garlic, minced

Salt

Rinse, stem, and seed the chiles. In an 8- to 10-inch frying pan over medium heat, stir the chiles in oil until they smell toasted, about 3 minutes, taking care not to scorch them. Pour the chiles from the pan into a blender. Add the garlic and 1/2 cup water. Purée the chiles until smooth. If desired, thin with 1 or more tablespoons water. Add salt to taste. Serve or cover and chill up to 1 day.

Makes about 1/2 cup

Tomatillo-Avocado Salsa for Beef

1/3 pound tomatillos

1/4 pound fresh jalapeño chiles

2 cloves garlic, peeled

1/2 cup lightly packed fresh cilantro

1 tablespoon olive oil

1 large firm-ripe avocado, pitted, peeled, and diced

1/2 cup minced onion

1 1/2 to 2 tablespoons fresh lime juice

Salt

Husk, rinse, and quarter the tomatillos. Rinse, stem, seed, and halve the jalapeño chiles. In a blender, coarsely purée the tomatillos, chiles, garlic, and cilantro. Pour the chile mixture into a bowl. Stir in the olive oil, avocado, and onion. Add the lime juice and salt to taste. Serve or cover and chill up to 1 day.

Makes about 2 1/2 cups

starters & sides

Romaine Hearts with Pipián

Prep and cook time: About 15 minutes

1 Discard the chile stems. Shake out and discard the chile seeds. Put the chiles in a bowl and pour 1 1/2 cups boiling water over them. Let stand until soft, 6 to 7 minutes.

2 Meanwhile, in an 8- to 10-inch frying pan over high heat, stir or shake the pumpkin seeds until they smell lightly toasted, 2 to 3 minutes.

3 Put the pumpkin seeds in a blender or food processor. Lift the chiles from the soaking liquid and add to the blender. Add the garlic, vinegar, tomatoes, and cilantro. Purée, adding enough chile-soaking liquid (about 1/2 cup) to make the pipián mixture thin enough to scoop but not drippy. Add salt to taste. Scrape the pipián into a small bowl.

4 Stand the romaine lettuce leaves, stem ends down, in a closely fitting bowl and drop ice cubes among the leaves to keep them crisp. Use the leaves as a scoop for the pipián dressing.

Makes about 8 servings

....

Notes from The Sunset Grill

Pipián is made in many parts of Mexico from a variety of dried corn, seeds, and chiles. Our version is made from puréed pumpkin seeds. Buy romaine hearts or use the tender inner leaves from the heads of romaine lettuce. The dressing can be made up to 1 day ahead— cover airtight and chill. Serve at room temperature.

3 dried California or New Mexico chiles (4 to 5 inches long)

1/2 cup shelled roasted pumpkin seeds (*pepitas*)

2 cloves garlic, peeled

2 tablespoons red wine vinegar

3/4 cup chopped Roma tomatoes

1/2 cup lightly packed fresh cilantro

Salt

24 to 32 romaine lettuce leaves (6 to 7 inches long), rinsed and crisped

Ice cubes

Sunchoke Dip

Prep and cook time: About 30 minutes

1 Peel the Jerusalem artichokes and rinse. In a 5- to 6-quart pan over high heat, bring 2 quarts water to a boil. Add the Jerusalem artichokes and cook until tender when pierced, about 12 minutes. Drain.

2 In a blender or food processor, purée the Jerusalem artichokes, garlic, lemon juice, and olive oil until smooth, scraping the container sides as needed. Add chiles and salt to taste. Scrape the dip into a bowl and serve with corn chips.

Makes about 8 servings

1¹/₂ pounds Jerusalem artichokes

2 cloves garlic, peeled

3 tablespoons fresh lemon juice

3 tablespoons extra-virgin olive oil

1 to 2 tablespoons minced fresh jalapeño chiles

Salt

Blue or red corn chips (or a combination; about 8 cups)

Notes from The Sunset Grill

Jerusalem artichokes (also known as sunchokes) are the root of a native American variety of sunflower.

Olive Oil
Essential to the Mediterranean kitchen, olive oil comes in several grades. The finest, extra virgin, comes from the olives' first cold pressing and is low in acid. Its distinctive flavor includes notes that can range from fruity to grassy to peppery. Use it to finish dishes, not for cooking, so these complex aromas can shine.

Roasted Tomatillo Guacamole

Prep and cook time: About 45 minutes

1 In a large frying pan over medium heat, brown the jalapeños, onion, garlic, and tomatillo on all sides, 20 to 25 minutes. Remove the vegetables to a plate as they finish browning.

2 In a blender or food processor, blend the vegetables with ¼ cup water just until chunky. Add the avocado and 1 tablespoon lime juice and pulse until blended. Scrape the mixture into a bowl. Stir in the cilantro, season to taste with salt, and add more lime juice if desired. Serve immediately.

Makes about 1¹/₂ cups

1 or 2 fresh jalapeños, stems removed, halved, and seeded

¹/₂ white onion, peeled

1 clove garlic, peeled

1 tomatillo, papery skin removed

1 ripe avocado, pitted, peeled, and cut into chunks

About 1 tablespoon fresh lime juice

¹/₃ cup loosely packed cilantro leaves, chopped

About ¹/₂ teaspoon salt

Tomatillos

Tart green tomatillos (literally "little tomato," though they're related to the Cape gooseberry) are essential to Mexican dishes like chile verde or green salsas. The fruit is encased in a papery husk, which must be removed before use. Fresh tomatillos are available at many supermarkets and Latino markets. Choose firm tomatillos with a fresh-looking husk.

Mushroom Bocadillos

Prep and cook time: About 1 1/4 hours

1 Preheat the oven to 325°F. Butter an 8-inch square baking dish. In a large frying pan over medium-high heat, melt 2 tablespoons butter. Add the mushrooms, onion, and nutmeg, stirring often until the mushrooms release their liquid and are lightly browned, about 10 minutes. Season to taste with salt and pepper and set aside to cool.

2 Meanwhile, in a bowl with a large fork, beat the eggs. Stir in the bread crumbs, cilantro, and all but 1/2 cup of the cheese. Coarsely chop the cooled mushroom mixture and stir it into the egg mixture. Pour the batter into the baking dish.

3 Bake until the batter is just set and the center feels firm when pressed, about 30 minutes. Sprinkle evenly with the remaining 1/2 cup cheese and bake just until the cheese begins to melt, 3 to 4 minutes more. Put the dish on a cooling rack and let cool about 15 minutes. Cut the bocadillos into 1-inch pieces, arrange on a platter, and serve warm.

Makes 8 servings

About 2 tablespoons butter, plus more for baking dish

1 pound button mushrooms, sliced

1/2 small onion, chopped

1/4 teaspoon ground nutmeg

Salt and freshly ground black pepper

4 eggs

1/4 cup fine dried bread crumbs

1/2 cup minced fresh cilantro

1/2 pound Monterey jack cheese, shredded

Notes from The Sunset Grill

Bocadillos means "little bites." You can make this dish up to 1 day ahead, cool, cover, and chill. Serve at room temperature or reheat, uncovered, in a 325°F oven until warm, about 10 minutes.

Spiedini di Mozzarella

Prep and cook time: About 40 minutes

1 Cut the bread into 12 slices about ¹/₂ inch thick. Lightly spread both sides of each slice with butter. Cut the cheese into ¹/₄-inch-thick slices.

2 Layer 3 bread slices with enough cheese between slices to cover the bread. Cut the stack into quarters. Push the cut end of a rosemary sprig through each quarter-stack of bread and cheese to hold the layers together. Repeat to use the remaining bread, cheese, and rosemary. If needed for stability, push toothpicks into stacks parallel to rosemary sprigs. Season to taste with salt and pepper.

3 Prepare a grill for cooking over high heat. First, oil the grill rack. If using a charcoal grill, prepare a solid bed of hot coals. If using a gas grill, preheat to high (you can hold your hand 1 to 2 inches above grill level only 2 to 3 seconds). Lay the skewered bread and cheese on the oiled grill rack. Close the lid if using a gas grill. Cook, turning often, until the bread is lightly toasted, 2 to 5 minutes. Serve immediately.

Makes 4 to 6 servings

About ³/₄ pound sourdough or other country-style bread

¹/₄ cup butter, at room temperature

³/₄ to 1 pound fresh mozzarella cheese

16 fresh rosemary sprigs (to use as skewers)

Salt and freshly ground black pepper

Grilled Oysters Mignonette

Prep and cook time: About 45 minutes

1   In a small bowl, combine the vinegar, lemon juice, horseradish, shallots, and sugar, whisking until blended. Season to taste with salt and pepper and set the sauce aside.

2   Prepare a grill for cooking over high heat. If using a charcoal grill, prepare a solid bed of hot coals. If using a gas grill, preheat to high (you can hold your hand 1 to 2 inches above grill level only 2 to 3 seconds). Put the oysters on the grill rack. Close the lid if using a gas grill. Cook just until the shells open, about 5 minutes. Remove from heat and serve immediately with the mignonette sauce.

Makes 4 servings

$1/2$ cup Champagne vinegar

$1/2$ cup fresh lemon juice

4 tablespoons freshly grated horseradish

4 tablespoons minced shallots

1 teaspoon sugar

Salt and freshly ground black pepper

2 dozen fresh oysters, rinsed

Notes from The Sunset Grill

Discard any oysters that haven't opened. We've found that West Coast varieties of oysters, such as Kumamotos and Olympias, have a creamy sweetness that's irresistible. Mignonette sauce is a classic accompaniment and can be used with grilled oysters or oysters on the half shell.

Wine-Steamed Mussels with Aioli

Prep and cook time: About 45 minutes

1   In a food processor, purée the egg yolks, mustard, salt, pepper, and 1 garlic clove until smooth. With the motor running, add the olive oil in a thin, steady stream until mixture is emulsified. Add the lemon juice and pulse to blend. Transfer the aioli to a bowl, cover, and chill until ready to serve.

2   In a 4-quart saucepan, combine the wine, the remaining 3 garlic cloves, and the onion. Bring to a boil over high heat, then reduce heat and simmer 5 minutes. Add the mussels, cover, and simmer until shells have opened, about 6 minutes.

3   With a slotted spoon, scoop the mussels from the pan into a serving bowl, discarding any that haven't opened. Whisk the butter into the wine mixture until melted, then stir in the parsley. Pour the sauce over the mussels and serve immediately with the aioli.

Makes 4 to 6 servings

....

Notes from The Sunset Grill

To drizzle the aioli over the mussels, put it in a sturdy plastic food bag, cut one corner of the bag, and squeeze the aioli over the mussels. Leftover aioli is excellent on sandwiches or blended with an avocado for a quick dip.

2 large egg yolks

2 teaspoons Dijon mustard

1/2 teaspoon kosher salt

1/2 teaspoon freshly ground black pepper

4 cloves garlic, peeled and crushed

1 cup mild extra-virgin olive oil

2 tablespoons fresh lemon juice

2 cups Pinot Gris or other dry white wine

1 onion, halved lengthwise, then thinly sliced

2 pounds mussels in shells, scrubbed and beards pulled off

2 tablespoons butter

1/2 cup finely chopped flat-leaf parsley

Chèvre and Mango Steak Bites

Prep and cook time: About 1¹/₂ hours

1 Trim any excess fat from the steak. Rinse the meat, pat dry, and rub it with the oil. Season the steak generously with salt and pepper.

2 Prepare a grill for cooking over high heat. First, oil the grill rack. If using a charcoal grill, prepare a solid bed of hot coals. If using a gas grill, preheat to high (you can hold your hand 1 to 2 inches above grill level only 2 to 3 seconds).

3 Lay the steak on the grill rack. If using a gas grill, close the lid. Cook the steak, turning once, until firm when pressed on thin end but still quite pink in the center (cut to test), about 4 minutes on each side. Transfer the steak to a platter, cover loosely with foil, and let cool at least 30 minutes. About 45 minutes before slicing, put steak in the freezer for easy slicing. Reserve the juices in the platter.

4 On a cutting board with a very sharp knife, cut the steak across the grain as thinly and evenly as possible, to make about 32 slices (save the narrow and uneven ends of the steak for another use). If the steak is wet, blot it with paper towels.

5 Combine the reserved meat juices with enough milk to measure 2 tablespoons and pour into a small bowl. Crumble the cheese into the bowl and mash it with a fork to make a smooth paste.

6 Working with 1 slice at a time, lay out the steak and spread it with ³/₄ teaspoon of the cheese mixture. Lay 1 mint leaf and 1 piece of mango at one end of the slice of steak and roll it up to make a bite. Repeat with the remaining ingredients. Let the bites stand at room temperature at least 10 minutes before serving.

Makes about 32 bites

1¹/₂ pounds beef flank steak

1 tablespoon olive oil

Salt and freshly ground black pepper

About 2 tablespoons milk

¹/₂ cup packed fresh goat cheese (about 4 ounces)

About 32 small mint leaves

About 15 dried mango pieces, cut into thin, 1-inch-long slices

....

Notes from The Sunset Grill
The finished bites can be covered and chilled for up to 6 hours.

Mango-Cucumber Salad

Prep time: About 20 minutes

In a small bowl, mix the vinegar, garlic, and curry paste. Put the cucumber, mango, radish, onion, basil, and mint in a medium bowl, then toss with the vinegar mixture to coat. Garnish with black sesame seeds. Serve immediately.

Makes 6 servings

....

Notes from The Sunset Grill
This salad has a fresh crunch and spicy kick. Serve it with grilled chicken or fish.

1 tablespoon seasoned rice wine vinegar

1 clove garlic, minced

1 teaspoon Thai green curry paste

1 English (seedless) cucumber, peeled and chopped

1 small mango, chopped

3/4 cup chopped red radish

1/4 cup chopped sweet onion

1 tablespoon chopped fresh basil

1 tablespoon chopped fresh mint

1/2 teaspoon black sesame seeds

Mango
The tropical mango is available in many supermarkets year-round. Look for ripe mangoes with red-blushed yellow skin, or ripen green fruit in a paper bag at room temperature. To cut mango easily, slice long pieces off the fruit, avoiding the large, flat seed; score flesh in a cross-hatch pattern; and cut off the peel.

Arugula-Avocado Salad

Prep time: About 20 minutes

1. In a small bowl, whisk together the oil and lemon juice to make the dressing. Add salt and pepper to taste. Set aside.

2. In a large salad bowl, combine the arugula, avocado, tomato, and hearts of palm. Toss with the dressing. Top with the pine nuts and cheese. Serve immediately.

Makes 4 to 6 servings

Notes from The Sunset Grill
If you can't find fresh hearts of palm, it's fine to use 2 canned hearts of palm, rinsed and chopped.

$^1/_4$ **cup extra-virgin olive oil**

2 tablespoons fresh lemon juice

Salt and freshly ground black pepper

6 ounces arugula leaves

1 avocado, pitted, peeled, and chopped

1 medium tomato, chopped

2 fresh hearts of palm (fibrous ends and leaves trimmed), chopped (see Notes)

$^1/_3$ **cup pine nuts, toasted (see below)**

2 tablespoons grated parmesan cheese

Toasting Pine Nuts
Lightly toasting pine nuts is a quick, easy way to lend them more intense, nutty flavor. To toast them, simply place the nuts in a small, dry frying pan over medium-high heat. Cook, stirring frequently or shaking the pan, until they are fragrant and light golden brown, 2 to 3 minutes. Let cool before using.

Tomato Salad with Chile and Lime

Prep time: About 25 minutes

1 Core and halve the tomatoes. Remove the seeds and cut the tomatoes into bite-size pieces. Put tomatoes in a large bowl.

2 Remove the stem and seeds from the chile. Finely chop the chile and add to the tomatoes. Set aside.

3 In a small bowl, whisk together the olive oil, lime juice, $^1/_2$ teaspoon salt, and mustard until emulsified. Drizzle the dressing over the tomatoes and chile, and toss gently to combine. Add more salt to taste if you like. Serve at room temperature.

Makes 8 servings

2 pounds ripe tomatoes

1 large mild green chile, such as poblano

3 tablespoons extra-virgin olive oil

2 tablespoons fresh lime juice

$^1/_2$ teaspoon salt, plus more to taste

$^1/_4$ teaspoon dry mustard

Notes from The Sunset Grill

Be sure to use ripe tomatoes—a variety of colors adds a nice touch—and good-quality olive oil for the best flavor. This salad fits nicely in a Mexican-themed buffet or on the table with beef fajitas or grilled pork or shrimp.

Heirloom Tomatoes

Heirloom tomato varieties like Brandywine, Cherokee Purple, and Green Zebra are widely available in summer at farmers' markets and produce stands. The seeds for these cultivars, produced by open pollination, were passed down over generations—hence the name. If you can't find heirloom tomatoes, substitute any vine-ripened tomato.

Three-Pepper Salad

Prep time: About 20 minutes

1. In a large bowl, combine the garlic and vinegar. Set aside to let the flavors blend, 15 minutes. Meanwhile, halve the peppers and remove the seeds and white membranes. Cut peppers into bite-size chunks and set aside. Separate the parsley leaves from stems. Discard the stems (you should have about 1 cup leaves). Finely chop the leaves and set aside.

2. Whisk the olive oil, 1/2 teaspoon salt, and 1/4 teaspoon pepper into the garlic-vinegar mixture. Add more salt and pepper to taste.

3. Toss the peppers, parsley, and onion with the dressing. Add the feta cheese and toss gently. Serve at room temperature, or cover and chill for up to 2 hours.

Makes 6 servings

1 clove garlic, minced

3 tablespoons Champagne vinegar

3 sweet bell peppers (red, orange, and yellow if possible; see Notes)

1/2 bunch flat-leaf parsley

2 tablespoons extra-virgin olive oil

1/2 teaspoon salt, plus more to taste

1/4 teaspoon freshly ground black pepper, plus more to taste

1/2 small red onion, peeled and sliced very thinly crosswise

1/2 cup crumbled feta cheese

Notes from The Sunset Grill

If you're using mini bell peppers, you'll need about 4 cups.

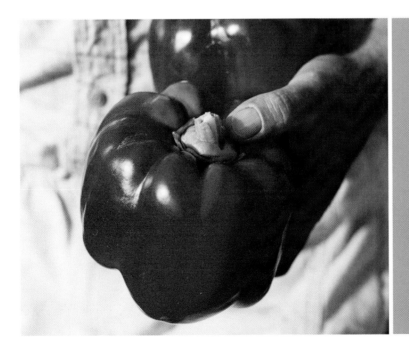

Bell Peppers

Sweet bell peppers, which come in a rainbow of colors, are in season in autumn, but imported peppers are available year-round in grocery stores. Red, yellow, and orange peppers are fully ripe and sweeter than the familiar but more immature green peppers. Look for smooth-skinned, shiny bell peppers that feel heavy for their size.

Roasted Beet Salad with Oranges and Queso Fresco

Prep and cook time: About 1¹/₂ hours, plus cooling time

1 Preheat the oven to 375°F. Scrub the beets, pat dry, rub with 1 tablespoon of the olive oil, and sprinkle generously with kosher salt. Put the beets on a foil-covered baking sheet and bake until tender when pierced, about 1 hour. Refrigerate uncovered until cool enough to handle, about 30 minutes (see Notes). Cut off the roots and stems, then rub the beets with paper towels to remove the skin; discard skin. Cut the beets in half lengthwise, then slice into half-moons about ¹/₄ inch thick; set aside.

2 Cut the ends off the oranges, then cut away peel and outer membrane in wide strips, following the curve of the fruit with the knife. Discard peel. Working over a bowl to catch the juices, cut the oranges between the inner membranes and the fruit to release segments into the bowl, then squeeze the juice from the membranes into the bowl and discard the membrane.

3 Hold the limes over another bowl and finely grate the zest. Juice the limes and add the juice to the zest. Add the shallots, vinegar, and juice from the oranges, keeping the orange segments separate. Whisking constantly, slowly drizzle the remaining 4 tablespoons olive oil into the bowl with the lime mixture. Add the beets, toss to coat, and season to taste with salt and pepper. Cover the bowls airtight and let stand at room temperature at least 15 minutes and up to 3 hours.

4 Arrange the arugula on a platter. Sprinkle with the cilantro leaves. Pour the beets and the dressing over the arugula and scatter with the orange segments and the cheese.

Makes 8 servings

....

Notes from The Sunset Grill

The beets can be roasted and cooled up to 3 days ahead. Queso fresco is a very mild fresh Mexican cheese carried by many supermarkets. If you can't find it, use a mild feta cheese.

4 beets (2¹/₂ inches wide, with root ends and stem ends intact), preferably a mixture of red, golden, and orange

5 tablespoons extra-virgin olive oil

Kosher salt

4 oranges

2 limes

2 tablespoons finely chopped shallots

2 tablespoons red wine vinegar

Freshly ground black pepper

6 cups arugula

¹/₂ cup fresh cilantro leaves

4 to 6 ounces queso fresco, crumbled (see Notes)

Grilled Asparagus with Orange and Parsley

Prep and cook time: About 30 minutes

1 Prepare a grill for cooking over medium-high heat. First, oil the grill rack. If using a charcoal grill, prepare a solid bed of medium-hot coals. If using a gas grill, preheat to high and close the lid, then open the lid and lower the heat to medium-high (you can hold your hand 1 to 2 inches above grill level only 3 to 4 seconds).

2 Meanwhile, snap off the stem end of the asparagus, where it naturally breaks when you bend it. Or to make the entire spear edible, trim away the very end, and peel the bottom half of the spear with a vegetable peeler. Stir together the orange zest, parsley, garlic, 2 tablespoons olive oil, and salt and pepper to taste. Set aside.

3 Toss the asparagus with some olive oil and salt, then lay the asparagus on the oiled grill rack. If using a gas grill, close the lid. Grill the asparagus, turning frequently, until tender and starting to brown, 3 to 4 minutes. Sprinkle with the orange-parsley mixture and serve hot or at room temperature.

Makes 4 servings

1 pound asparagus

Finely grated zest from 1 orange

2 tablespoons chopped flat-leaf parsley

1 small clove garlic, minced

2 tablespoons olive oil, plus more for grilling asparagus

Salt and freshly ground black pepper

Grilled Artichokes with Green Olive Dip

Prep and cook time: About 1 hour

1 Slice the tops off the artichokes, pull off the small leaves, trim the stems, and snip off the thorny tips. In a large pot, bring 1 to 2 inches of water to a boil. Add 1 tablespoon salt, 2 tablespoons of the lemon juice, and the artichokes; cover and steam until the artichoke bottoms pierce easily, 20 to 40 minutes. Drain the artichokes. When cool enough to handle, cut each in half lengthwise and scrape out the fuzzy center.

2 Meanwhile, prepare a grill for cooking over medium heat. First, oil the grill rack. If using a charcoal grill, prepare a solid bed of medium coals. If using a gas grill, preheat to high and close the lid, then open the lid and lower the heat to medium (you can hold your hand 1 to 2 inches above grill level only 4 to 5 seconds).

3 Prepare the Green Olive Dip: In a blender, mix the parsley, olive oil, chopped green olives, capers, lemon juice, mustard, pepper, and salt until chunky. Spoon into a bowl and set aside.

4 In another bowl, combine the garlic, olive oil, the remaining 2 tablespoons lemon juice, $1/2$ teaspoon salt, and the pepper. Brush the artichokes with the garlic mixture and set, cut side down, on the oiled grill rack. Grill, turning once, until lightly browned, about 5 minutes on each side.

5 Serve the artichokes immediately, with the Green Olive Dip alongside.

Makes 6 servings

6 artichokes

1 tablespoon plus $1/2$ teaspoon salt

4 tablespoons fresh lemon juice

3 cloves garlic, minced

3 tablespoons extra-virgin olive oil

$1/4$ teaspoon freshly ground black pepper

GREEN OLIVE DIP

$1/2$ cup chopped flat-leaf parsley

5 tablespoons extra-virgin olive oil

2 tablespoons chopped green olives, such as Picholine

1 tablespoon drained capers

1 tablespoon fresh lemon juice

$1/2$ teaspoon Dijon mustard

$1/4$ teaspoon freshly ground black pepper

$1/8$ teaspoon salt

Bacon-Olive Potato Salad

Prep and cook time: About 30 minutes

1   Rinse and scrub the potatoes. Halve lengthwise and cut them into ¼-inch slices. Put the potatoes in a large pot, cover with cold water, and bring to a boil. Add the salt, reduce the heat to maintain a slow boil, and cook the potatoes until tender to the bite, about 8 minutes. Drain the potatoes and put in a large bowl.

2   Meanwhile, in a large frying pan (not nonstick) over medium-high heat, cook the bacon until brown and crisp. Add the vinegar and, using a wooden spoon, scrape up any browned bits on the bottom of the pan. Keep the bacon warm over low heat.

3   In a food processor, pulse the olives, shallots, and capers until chopped. Add the bacon to the olive mixture, stir, and pour over the potatoes. Add the parsley and toss to combine. Taste for seasoning and serve warm or at room temperature.

Makes 6 to 8 servings

2 pounds red-skinned potatoes

1 tablespoon salt

½ pound thick-cut bacon, chopped

¼ cup cider vinegar

⅔ cup pitted picholine olives

⅔ cup pitted kalamata olives

4 large shallots, peeled

3 tablespoons brined capers

2 tablespoons chopped flat-leaf parsley

....

Notes from The Sunset Grill
This warm potato salad goes well with grilled chicken or pork. It can be held at room temperature for up to an hour.

Olives
Briny green and meaty black olives each add distinct notes to this potato salad. Picholines, green olives from the south of France, are firm fleshed and elongated. Greek Kalamata olives have a purple-black hue. They are small, but strong in taste and pleasantly salty.

Classic American Potato Salad

Prep and cook time: About 1 hour

1 Put the eggs in a pot and cover with cold water. Bring to a boil, cover, remove from the heat, and let the eggs sit in the covered pot for 14 minutes. Transfer the eggs to a large bowl of ice water for at least 10 minutes or until you are ready to use, up to 1 hour.

2 Peel the potatoes and cut them into bite-size pieces. Put the potatoes in a large pot, cover with cold water, and bring to a boil. Add 1 tablespoon salt, reduce the heat to maintain a slow boil, and cook the potatoes until tender to the bite, about 8 minutes. Drain the potatoes, put them in a large bowl, and toss with the vinegar. Let them cool to room temperature, about 30 minutes.

3 Meanwhile, finely chop the onion and set aside. Finely chop the celery, pickles, and parsley. In a bowl, mix the mayonnaise, onion, celery, pickles, parsley, mustard, pepper, and remaining 1/2 teaspoon salt. Peel and chop the eggs.

4 Gently toss the cooled potatoes with the dressing. Gently mix in the eggs. Serve immediately.

Makes 6 to 8 servings

3 eggs

2 pounds russet potatoes

1 tablespoon plus 1/2 teaspoon salt

3 tablespoons white wine vinegar

1/2 small red onion

1 large celery stalk

1/2 cup bread-and-butter pickle slices

1/2 cup flat-leaf parsley leaves

1/2 cup mayonnaise

1/2 teaspoon Dijon mustard

1/4 teaspoon freshly ground black pepper

....

Notes from The Sunset Grill
This salad is at its best right after it's made, but can be kept, covered and chilled, for up to 2 days.

Chipotle Coleslaw

Prep time: About 30 minutes, plus 30 minutes to chill

1 In a medium bowl, stir together the mayonnaise, sour cream, vinegar, molasses, sugar, minced chile, adobo sauce, and 1 teaspoon salt.

2 In a large bowl, toss together the green and red cabbage, the green onions, and 3/4 cup chopped cilantro. Pour the dressing over the vegetables, toss well, and refrigerate for at least 30 minutes and up to 4 hours. Before serving, add more salt to taste and scatter the remaining 1/4 cup chopped cilantro over the top.

Makes 6 to 8 servings

....

Notes from The Sunset Grill

This is delicious piled atop Spiced Pulled-Pork Sandwiches, page 163.

1/2 cup mayonnaise

1/2 cup sour cream

3 tablespoons white vinegar

1 tablespoon molasses (not blackstrap)

1 1/2 teaspoons sugar

1 small canned chipotle chile, minced, plus 2 teaspoons adobo sauce from the can

1 teaspoon kosher salt, plus more to taste

6 cups packed shredded green cabbage

6 cups packed shredded red cabbage

7 green onions, green and pale green portions, sliced into thin rounds

1 cup tightly packed chopped fresh cilantro leaves

Cilantro
Feathery-leaved cilantro—also known as fresh coriander—adds a dusky herbal note to foods and is particularly popular in Asian and Latin American cuisines. Its bright flavor quickly evaporates with heat, so it is best used in uncooked dishes or added at the end of cooking.

Santa Fe Corn Pudding

Prep and cook time: About 1 1/4 hours

1 Preheat the oven to 350°F. Butter a 2-quart baking dish using melted butter.

2 Put 1 3/4 cups corn kernels in the bowl of a food processor. Pulse until the mixture is puréed but still a bit chunky, about 5 pulses. Set aside.

3 In a large bowl, whisk together the eggs, half-and-half, and 1 teaspoon salt. Add both the whole and puréed corn kernels, the green chiles, 1/4 cup crackers, and 3 tablespoons melted butter. Stir to combine. Spoon the mixture into the prepared baking dish and scatter cheese over the top.

4 In a small bowl, mix together the remaining 3/4 cup cracker crumbs and 1 tablespoon melted butter. Sprinkle over the cheese.

5 Bake the pudding until puffed and golden brown, about 45 to 50 minutes. The edges should be a bit crusty and the center still a little jiggly. Serve immediately.

Makes 6 to 8 servings

4 tablespoons melted butter, plus more for the baking dish

4 cups fresh corn kernels (from about 6 ears)

2 large eggs

1 1/2 cups half-and-half

1 teaspoon kosher salt, plus more to taste

1/2 cup chopped roasted green chiles (see Notes)

1 cup crushed good-quality buttery salted crackers

1/2 cup grated Monterey jack cheese or pepper jack cheese

Notes from The Sunset Grill

This savory, custardy pudding is best when corn is at its ripest, but it can also be made with frozen corn. Fresh or frozen roasted green chiles (such as Anaheim or New Mexico varieties) will give the dish more flavor, but if these aren't available, you can substitute canned roasted green chiles. Try to find crackers made with real butter.

Spicy Baked Beans

Prep and cook time: About 1 1/2 hours

1 Preheat the oven to 350°F. Rub a 2 1/2- to 3-quart baking dish with oil.

2 In a large skillet over medium heat, cook the bacon until beginning to brown but still limp. Stir in the onion and cook until soft and translucent and the bacon is crisp, about 5 minutes more. Spoon the mixture into the prepared baking dish. Add the baked beans, chili sauce, Worcestershire sauce, mustard, paprika, and cumin. Stir, taste to check seasonings, and add salt if you like.

3 Bake the beans, uncovered, until bubbly throughout with a bit of browned crust around the edges of the dish, about 45 minutes. Serve immediately.

Makes 6 to 8 servings

....

Notes from The Sunset Grill

Chili sauce is sold in ketchup-style bottles in the supermarket condiment aisle.

Oil for baking dish

7 ounces bacon, diced

1 large onion, finely chopped

2 cans (28 ounces each) barbecue-flavor baked beans

1/4 cup bottled chili sauce (see Notes)

2 tablespoons Worcestershire sauce

2 tablespoons prepared yellow mustard

1 1/2 tablespoons smoked paprika

1/2 teaspoon ground cumin

Kosher salt (optional)

Ground Paprika

Paprika comes in many varieties, from mild to hot. The smoked variety called for here comes from Spain, where it is called *pimentón* and may be mild *(dulce)*, medium, or hot. Look for smoked Spanish paprika in specialty food shops, some supermarkets, or online; if you can't find it, flavorful Hungarian-style paprika may be substituted.

Grilled Green-Onion Breads

Prep and cook time: About 15 minutes, plus 1¼ hours to rise

1 With your hands, flatten the bread dough on a floured board. Top with the olive oil and green onions and knead into the dough until incorporated (the dough will be sticky).

2 Place the dough in a bowl and cover. Let the dough rise in a warm place until doubled, 50 to 60 minutes.

3 On a floured board, knead the dough briefly to get out the air. Divide the dough into 12 equal pieces. Roll each piece into a ball and coat with some flour. Shape each ball into a 4- to 5-inch round, sprinkling with flour as needed to prevent sticking. Space the rounds evenly on two floured 15- by 17-inch baking sheets. Cover loosely with a kitchen towel and let rise until puffy, 20 to 30 minutes.

4 Meanwhile, prepare a grill for cooking over medium heat. First, oil the grill rack. If using a charcoal grill, prepare a solid bed of medium coals. If using a gas grill, preheat to high and close the lid, then open the lid and lower the heat to medium (you can hold your hand 1 to 2 inches above grill level only 4 to 5 seconds).

5 Lay the rounds of dough on the oiled grill rack. Cook, turning once, until the breads are browned, about 3 minutes on each side. Transfer the breads to a basket. Serve hot (cover with foil to keep warm up to 30 minutes) or cool.

Makes 12 flatbreads

....

Notes from The Sunset Grill
These breads are delicious served with Tamil Chicken Wings, page 119.

1 loaf (1 pound) frozen white or whole-wheat bread dough, thawed to room temperature

3 tablespoons extra-virgin olive oil

¾ cup sliced green onions

About ⅓ cup all-purpose flour

fish & shellfish

FISH

SHELLFISH

Swordfish Kebabs with Poblano Chiles

Prep and cook time: About 30 minutes, plus 30 minutes to marinate

1 Place the onion, lemon juice, 2 tablespoons olive oil, garlic, salt, cumin, paprika, peppercorns, and crushed red pepper in a food processor and process until smooth. Combine the marinade and swordfish in a bowl, cover, and refrigerate 30 minutes. Meanwhile, soak 8 (12-inch) wooden skewers in water to cover for 30 minutes.

2 Prepare a grill for cooking over medium-high heat. First, oil the grill rack. If using a charcoal grill, prepare a solid bed of medium-hot coals. If using a gas grill, preheat to high and close the lid, then open the lid and lower the heat to medium-high (you can hold your hand 1 to 2 inches above grill level only 3 to 4 seconds).

3 Remove the swordfish from the bowl, reserving the marinade. Thread the fish pieces, cherry tomatoes, and poblano chiles alternately onto the soaked skewers. Lay the skewers on the grill rack. If using a gas grill, close the lid.

4 Cook 10 minutes or until the fish flakes easily when tested with a fork, turning and basting frequently with the reserved marinade. Serve immediately, on or off the skewers.

Makes 4 servings

....

Notes from The Sunset Grill
Try serving these kebabs with rice pilaf or wrapped in warm pita bread.

1 cup chopped onion

1/4 cup fresh lemon juice (about 2 lemons)

About 2 tablespoons olive oil

1 tablespoon minced garlic

1 teaspoon salt

1 teaspoon ground cumin

1 teaspoon paprika

1/2 teaspoon black peppercorns

1/4 teaspoon crushed red pepper

1 pound swordfish, cut into 1/2-inch cubes

1 pint large cherry tomatoes

4 poblano chiles, seeded and cut into 1-inch pieces

Fish Tacos with Relish, Salsa, and Slaw

Prep and cook time: About 45 minutes

1 Prepare the Corn-Avocado Relish, Salsa Fresca, and Easy Garden Slaw. For the relish, in a large bowl, whisk together the lime juice, vinegar, olive oil, salt, pepper, cumin, and cayenne. Remove the husks and silk from the corn. Cut the kernels off the cobs (about 2 cups) and add to the bowl. Stem, seed, and dice the red pepper. Add the diced pepper, onion, and cilantro to the bowl and stir into the dressing. Pit, peel, and chop the avocados. Add to the bowl and gently mix, taking care not to smash the avocado.

For the salsa, in a large bowl, mix together the tomatoes, onion, and chopped chile to taste. Add the lime juice and salt to taste.

For the slaw, in a large bowl, whisk together the vinegar, cream, salt, celery salt, and pepper. Add the shredded cabbage and the carrots and mix well.

2 Rinse the fish and pat dry. Peel the onions and cut lengthwise into quarters, keeping the root ends intact. Brush both sides of the fish fillets and the onion quarters with oil. Sprinkle evenly with salt and pepper. Stack the tortillas and wrap in foil.

3 Set the tortillas and onions on an oiled barbecue grill over medium-hot coals or medium-high heat on a gas grill (you can hold your hand 1 to 2 inches above grill level only 3 to 4 seconds); close lid on gas grill. Cook the tortillas until hot, turning 2 or 3 times, 10 to 15 minutes total. Cook the onions, turning once, until cooked through and lightly charred, 10 to 15 minutes total.

4 Grill the fish, turning once, until barely opaque in center of thickest part (cut to test), 6 to 8 minutes total.

5 Arrange the fish, onions, and lime wedges on a platter or divide among plates. Place the warm tortillas in a napkin-lined basket. Offer the relish, salsa, and slaw for guests to add to taste.

Makes 8 servings

4 pounds boned and skinned tilapia fillets or other firm, white-fleshed fish fillets

4 red onions

About 1/4 cup olive oil

1 teaspoon salt

1/2 teaspoon freshly ground black pepper

24 to 32 white corn tortillas (6-inch)

Lime wedges

CORN-AVOCADO RELISH

1/4 cup fresh lime juice

1 tablespoon red wine vinegar

1 tablespoon olive oil

1 1/2 teaspoons salt

1/2 teaspoon freshly ground black pepper

1/4 teaspoon ground cumin

1/8 teaspoon cayenne

2 ears corn

1 red bell pepper

1/2 cup diced red onion

1/4 cup chopped fresh cilantro

3 firm-ripe avocados

SALSA FRESCA

4 firm-ripe tomatoes, cored, seeded, and chopped

1/2 cup diced red onion

2 to 3 tablespoons chopped jalapeño chile

1 tablespoon fresh lime juice

1 to 1 1/2 teaspoons salt

EASY GARDEN SLAW

5 tablespoons malt vinegar

1 tablespoon heavy cream

1 teaspoon salt

1/2 teaspoon celery salt

1/2 teaspoon freshly ground black pepper

8 cups shredded green cabbage

2 carrots, peeled and grated

Grilled Halibut with Sweet Peppers and Herbs

Prep and cook time: About 1 hour

1 Prepare a grill for cooking over medium-high heat. First, oil the grill rack. If using a charcoal grill, prepare a solid bed of medium-hot coals. If using a gas grill, preheat to high and close the lid, then open the lid and lower the heat to medium-high (you can hold your hand 1 to 2 inches above grill level only 3 to 4 seconds).

2 Meanwhile, cut both the red and yellow peppers in half lengthwise, and discard the seeds and membranes. Place pepper halves, skin side down, on a cutting board or work surface and flatten with your hand. When the grill is ready, place the pepper halves on it and grill, turning once, until blackened on both sides, about 12 minutes. Place in a resealable plastic bag and seal. Let stand 10 minutes.

3 Peel the bell peppers and cut into strips. Combine them with 2 tablespoons parsley, 2 tablespoons chives, vinegar, 1 tablespoon oil, capers, marjoram, 1/4 teaspoon salt, 1/4 teaspoon pepper, and garlic. Toss gently to coat and set aside.

4 Sprinkle the fish evenly with the remaining 1/2 teaspoon salt and remaining 1/4 teaspoon black pepper. Lay the fish on the grill rack. If using a gas grill, close the lid. Grill, turning once, until fish is opaque throughout, about 5 minutes on each side. Sprinkle the fish with the remaining 1 tablespoon parsley and 1 tablespoon chives. Serve with the bell pepper mixture.

Makes 4 servings

....

Notes from The Sunset Grill

This sweet-pepper salad pairs well with halibut, snapper, or other firm, white-fleshed fish. You can also serve it with grilled chicken breast or pork tenderloin.

2 red bell peppers

2 yellow bell peppers

3 tablespoons finely chopped fresh flat-leaf parsley

3 tablespoons finely chopped fresh chives

2 tablespoons white balsamic vinegar

About 1 tablespoon extra-virgin olive oil

1 tablespoon capers

1 teaspoon finely chopped fresh marjoram

3/4 teaspoon salt

1/2 teaspoon freshly ground black pepper

1 clove garlic, minced

4 halibut fillets (about 6 ounces each)

Whole Striped Bass in Leaves

Prep and cook time: About 1½ hours

1 Rinse the fish and pat dry. Arrange the lemon and onion slices in the fish cavity and sprinkle the fish with salt and pepper. Oil both sides of a hinged wire basket. Line the bottom of the basket by overlapping about 12 grape leaves. Place the fish on top of the grape leaves, top evenly with the bay leaves, then cover with the remaining grape leaves. Close the basket and secure tightly. Sprinkle water on the grape leaves on each side of the basket.

2 Prepare a grill for cooking over medium heat. First, oil the grill rack. If using a charcoal grill, prepare a solid bed of medium coals. If using a gas grill, preheat to high and close the lid, then open the lid and lower the heat to medium (you can hold your hand 1 to 2 inches above grill level only 4 to 5 seconds). Place the basket with fish on the grill rack 4 to 6 inches above the coals. If using a gas grill, close the lid.

3 Cook, turning the basket every 15 minutes, until the fish is opaque throughout, about 45 minutes. Push the grape leaves away with a fork to test.

4 Open the basket and peel off and discard the grape leaves, bay leaves, and top layer of skin. Slide the fish without the leaves onto a cutting board. Cut along the backbone to loosen the top fillet. Slide a wide metal spatula between the flesh and rib bones, and lift off the fillet. Place the fillet on a warm platter. Lift away the backbone and rib bones and discard the lemon and onion slices. Remove the bottom fillet and place it on the platter, leaving the skin behind. Garnish with the lemon wedges and fresh bay leaves.

Makes 8 to 10 servings

1 whole striped bass (6 to 8 pounds), cleaned, scaled, and head removed if desired

2 lemons, cut into ¼-inch-thick slices, plus lemon wedges for serving

2 small onions, cut into ¼-inch-thick slices

Salt and freshly ground black pepper

Olive oil for oiling wire basket

About 24 fresh grape leaves

5 or 6 fresh bay leaves, plus more for serving

Notes from The Sunset Grill

Wrapping a whole fish—such as striped bass, snapper, or salmon—in grape leaves imparts flavor and helps to keep it moist during cooking.

Salmon Trout with Prosciutto and Fennel

Prep and cook time: About 1 hour

1 Prepare a grill for cooking over medium-high heat. First, oil the grill rack. If using a charcoal grill, prepare a solid bed of medium-hot coals. If using a gas grill, preheat to high and close the lid, then open the lid and lower the heat to medium-high (you can hold your hand 1 to 2 inches above grill level only 3 to 4 seconds).

2 Brush the fish evenly with 2 teaspoons of the olive oil and sprinkle with 1/4 teaspoon salt and 1/8 teaspoon pepper. Combine 2 teaspoons olive oil and 2 tablespoons of the lemon juice. Set aside.

3 Remove the fennel fronds from the bulbs and chop the fronds. You will need 1/4 cup chopped fronds. In a bowl, combine 1/8 teaspoon pepper, the prosciutto, fennel fronds, fennel seeds, and garlic, stirring well. Heat the remaining 5 teaspoons olive oil in a large nonstick skillet over medium-high heat. Sauté the prosciutto mixture until crisp, about 3 minutes.

4 Cut the fennel bulbs vertically in half and cut away the tough cores. Place the fennel bulbs on the grill rack and grill until golden brown and tender, about 4 minutes on each side. Cut into 1/4-inch-thick slices and keep warm.

5 Lay the fish on the grill rack. If using a gas grill, close the lid. Grill until opaque throughout, turning once, about 5 minutes on each side, basting occasionally with the lemon juice mixture. Transfer the fish to a serving platter and sprinkle evenly with the remaining 1/4 teaspoon salt and 1/4 teaspoon pepper. Top with the prosciutto mixture and drizzle with the remaining 2 tablespoons lemon juice. Serve immediately with the grilled fennel and lemon wedges.

Makes 4 servings

Notes from The Sunset Grill
If you can't find salmon trout, you can use regular trout instead.

2 skin-on salmon trout fillets (about 8 ounces each)

About 3 tablespoons olive oil

1/2 teaspoon salt

1/2 teaspoon freshly ground black pepper

1/4 cup fresh lemon juice

1/2 cup (2 ounces) finely chopped prosciutto

2 fennel bulbs

1/8 teaspoon fennel seeds, crushed

2 cloves garlic, minced

4 lemon wedges

Grilled Salmon with Blackberry-Cabernet Coulis

Prep and cook time: About 45 minutes

1 In a food processor or blender, combine the wine and 2 cups berries and process until puréed. Rub the berry mixture through a fine strainer into a 1 1/2- to 2-quart pan and discard the residue. Add the shallots, ginger, and 2 tablespoons sugar. Bring the berry mixture to a boil over high heat, and stir often until reduced to 1 cup, about 10 minutes. Remove from heat and stir in butter and more sugar to taste (see Notes).

2 Rinse the salmon and pat dry. Coil the belly strips of fish into the center of the steaks and secure each portion with a small wooden skewer.

3 Prepare a grill for cooking over high heat. First, oil the grill rack. If using a charcoal grill, prepare a solid bed of hot coals. If using a gas grill, preheat to high (you can hold your hand 1 to 2 inches above grill level only 2 to 3 seconds). Lay the salmon on the grill rack. If using a gas grill, close the lid. Cook the fish, turning once, until opaque but still moist-looking in center of thickest part (cut to test), 7 to 10 minutes.

4 Set a salmon steak on each of 6 warm plates and remove the skewers. Spoon the berry coulis (if cool, stir over high heat until warm, about 1 minute) over the steaks. Garnish with the remaining 1/2 cup whole berries and season with salt and pepper to taste.

Makes 6 servings

....

Notes from The Sunset Grill
The berry sauce should be nicely balanced between sweet and tart.
Judge the amount of sugar to add by the sweetness of the fruit.

1 cup Cabernet Sauvignon or other dry red wine

2 1/2 cups blackberries, rinsed and drained

2 tablespoons minced shallots

2 tablespoons minced fresh ginger

2 to 3 tablespoons sugar

1 tablespoon butter

6 salmon steaks (1 inch thick, 6 to 7 ounces each)

Salt and freshly ground black pepper

Crisp-Skin Grilled Salmon

Prep and cook time: About 45 minutes

1 Prepare a gas or charcoal grill for indirect heat. If using a gas grill, turn all burners to high and close the lid. When the temperature inside the grill reaches 400°F, lift the lid and turn off one of the burners, creating the indirect heat area. If using a charcoal grill, light 50 to 60 briquets and let burn until just covered with ash, 20 to 30 minutes. Mound them to one side, leaving a cleared area for indirect cooking.

2 Fold two 12- by 18-inch pieces of heavy-duty aluminum foil in half widthwise to form rectangles. Using the tip of a small knife, keeping the foil folded, make holes in the rectangles about 2 inches apart and widen each hole to the size of a dime. Rub the folded foil with olive oil and set over direct heat for 2 minutes.

3 Meanwhile, rinse and dry the salmon fillets. Brush the skins with olive oil and set 2 fillets, skin side down, on each folded foil rectangle. Cover the grill (if using charcoal, open vents on lid) and cook the fish until the skin is light brown and really sizzling, 5 to 6 minutes. Slide the foil to indirect heat, cover, and cook until all but the top 1/4 inch is cooked, 3 to 8 minutes. Slide the fish back over direct heat, cover, and cook until the fish is cooked through (cut to test) and the skin is browned and crisp, about 3 minutes.

4 Transfer the foil with the salmon to a baking sheet and, sliding an offset cake spatula or other thin spatula between salmon skin and foil, very gently free the fish from the foil. Season with kosher salt, black pepper, and a few drops of lemon juice.

Makes 4 servings

Olive oil

4 center-cut skin-on salmon fillets (6 to 8 ounces each)

Kosher salt

Freshly ground black pepper

Fresh lemon juice

Sweet-Cured and Smoked Salmon

Prep and cook time: About 2 hours, plus 3 hours for curing

1 In a medium bowl, mix the salt, 1 cup brown sugar, 3 tablespoons garlic powder, 3 tablespoons onion powder, 1 tablespoon savory, 2 teaspoons dried tarragon, and all of the dill weed. Set aside. Rinse the salmon and pat dry. Set the salmon, skin side down, in an 11- by 17-inch roasting pan lined with plastic wrap. Spread the salt mixture evenly over the flesh of salmon. Cover and chill 3 hours.

2 Rinse the fish under cool water and pat dry. Set the fillet, skin side down, on a large sheet of foil. Cut the foil to fit the outline of the fish. Let the fish stand until the flesh is sticky to the touch, 20 to 30 minutes. Meanwhile, in a small bowl, mix the remaining 2 tablespoons brown sugar, 1 1/2 teaspoons garlic powder, 1 1/2 teaspoons onion powder, 1/2 teaspoon savory, and 1/2 teaspoon tarragon. Set aside.

3 In a large bowl, pour warm water over the wood chips to cover. Let them soak for at least 15 minutes. Prepare a grill for cooking over indirect heat. First, oil the grill rack. If using a charcoal grill, light 50 to 60 briquets and let burn until covered with ash, about 20 to 30 minutes. Push half of the coals to each side, leaving the center clear. If using a gas grill, turn all burners to high and close the lid. When the temperature inside the grill reaches 350° to 400°F, lift the lid, turn off one of the burners for the indirect-heat area, and lower the other burner(s) to medium.

4 Drain the wood chips. For the charcoal grill, scatter half of the chips on each mound of coals. If using a gas grill, put the chips in a foil pan and set directly on heat. Cover the grill (if using charcoal, open vents on lid) and heat until chips start to smolder, about 10 minutes. Set the grill rack 4 to 6 inches above the firegrate.

5 Lay the salmon, still on the foil, in the center of the grill rack (not directly over heat). Sprinkle the sugar mixture evenly over the fish. Cover the grill (if using charcoal, open vents on lid) and cook the salmon until a thermometer inserted in the center of the thickest part reaches 140°F, 20 to 25 minutes. Using two wide spatulas, slide the fillet with the foil onto a platter. Tuck the edges of foil under the fillet and serve.

Makes 8 servings

1 cup salt

1 cup plus 2 tablespoons firmly packed light brown sugar

3 tablespoons plus 1 1/2 teaspoons garlic powder

3 tablespoons plus 1 1/2 teaspoons onion powder

1 tablespoon plus 1/2 teaspoon dried savory

2 1/2 teaspoons dried tarragon

1 tablespoon dried dill weed

1 whole salmon fillet (about 3 pounds)

1 cup alder, apple, or mesquite wood chips

Planked Salmon

Prep and cook time: About 1 hour, plus at least 1 hour to marinate

1 In a container just wide and long enough to hold the plank, combine 2 parts water and 1 part Pinot Noir. Rinse the plank and immerse it in the Pinot Noir mixture for at least 1 hour or up to 1 day. About 30 minutes before cooking, immerse the fish in the red wine mixture with the plank. In another container, soak the wood chips in 2 to 3 cups of the red wine mixture.

2 Prepare a grill for cooking over indirect heat. First, oil the grill rack. If using a charcoal grill, light 50 to 60 briquets and let burn until covered with ash, about 20 to 30 minutes, then push equal amounts to opposite sides of the firegrate. Add 5 more briquets to each mound of coals. Set the oiled grill rack in place. If using a gas grill, turn all burners to high and close the lid. When the temperature inside the grill reaches 350° to 400°F, lift the lid, turn off one of the burners, and lower the other burner(s) to medium.

3 Drain the wood chips. Sprinkle them onto the hot coals. Or, if using a gas grill, put the chips in a smoke box or foil pan directly on the heat in a corner as grill heats. Lift the fish and plank from the wine mixture. Lay the fish on the plank, skin side down, season with salt and pepper, and top with 3 sprigs *each* of rosemary, marjoram, and thyme. Set the grill rack in place. Set the plank and the fish on the grill between the coals or gas heat. Cover the grill (open vents if using charcoal) and cook the fish until it is barely opaque but still moist-looking in the center of the thickest part (cut to test), 25 to 30 minutes. (If the plank chars, squirt or mop the dark areas with water.)

4 Set the plank with the fish on the table. Replace the scorched herbs with fresh ones and garnish the fish with lemon. Serve the salmon with more lemon wedges alongside.

Makes 6 servings

2 to 4 cups Pinot Noir

An untreated wood plank, about 1 x 8 x 18 inches

1 whole salmon fillet (about 18 inches long, $2^1/4$ to $2^1/2$ pounds)

2 cups alder or mesquite wood chips

Salt and freshly ground black pepper

6 rosemary sprigs

6 marjoram sprigs

6 thyme sprigs

Lemon wedges

Grilled Tuna and Barley with Lemon and Mint

Prep and cook time: About 1 hour, plus 30 minutes to marinate

1   Combine 1/2 cup mint, the lemon zest, 4 teaspoons lemon juice, 1/4 teaspoon salt, red pepper, and garlic in a shallow dish. Add the tuna, turning to coat. Cover and refrigerate 30 minutes.

2   Meanwhile, combine 1/4 teaspoon salt and 2 1/4 cups water in a medium saucepan and bring to a boil. Stir in the barley, cover, reduce heat, and simmer until the barley is tender and the liquid is absorbed, about 30 minutes. Remove from the heat, cover, and let stand 5 minutes. Spoon the barley into a large bowl and let cool slightly. Mix in the remaining 1/4 cup mint, the tomato, green onions, capers, and olives. Set aside.

3   In a small bowl, combine the remaining 1/4 teaspoon salt, 2 tablespoons lemon juice, and 1 tablespoon olive oil, stirring well with a whisk. Drizzle over the barley mixture and toss gently to coat. Set aside.

4   Prepare a grill for cooking over medium-high heat. First, oil the grill rack. If using a charcoal grill, prepare a solid bed of medium-hot coals. If using a gas grill, preheat to high and close the lid, then open the lid and lower the heat to medium-high (you can hold your hand 1 to 2 inches above grill level only 3 to 4 seconds). Lay the tuna on the grill rack. If using a gas grill, close the lid. Cook the tuna steaks, turning once, until medium-rare, about 4 minutes on each side.

5   Divide the barley mixture among 4 plates and set a tuna steak alongside.

Makes 4 servings

3/4 cup finely chopped fresh mint

1 teaspoon grated lemon zest

3 tablespoons plus 1 teaspoon fresh lemon juice

3/4 teaspoon salt

1/2 teaspoon crushed red pepper

3 cloves garlic, minced

4 Yellowfin tuna steaks (about 6 ounces each)

1 cup uncooked pearl barley

2 cups chopped tomato

3/4 cup chopped green onions

2 tablespoons capers

2 tablespoons chopped pitted kalamata olives

About 1 tablespoon extra-virgin olive oil

Garlic Butterflied Shrimp

Prep and cook time: About 45 minutes

1 Prepare the Salsa Cruda and set aside. Cut each shrimp down the back, from neck to tail, almost all the way through. Rinse the shrimp and lay it open, cut side down, pressing gently to flatten. For easier handling and to hold the shrimp flat, run thin metal skewers, in parallel pairs, crosswise through shrimp, filling the skewers.

2 In a 6- to 8-inch frying pan over low heat, stir the butter and garlic occasionally until the butter melts, about 4 minutes. Remove from the heat. Mix or brush the shrimp with 2/3 cup of the butter mixture.

3 Prepare a grill for cooking over high heat. First, oil the grill rack. If using a charcoal grill, prepare a solid bed of hot coals. If using a gas grill, preheat to high (you can hold your hand 1 to 2 inches above grill level only 2 to 3 seconds). Lay the skewered shrimp on the grill rack. If using a gas grill, close the lid. Cook, turning once, until the shrimp are opaque but still moist-looking in the thickest part (cut to test), 5 to 7 minutes. Transfer the cooked shrimp to a plate. While the shrimp are cooling, warm the flour tortillas on the grill.

4 Warm the remaining garlic butter and spoon over the shrimp. Season with salt, pepper, and lime to taste. Wrap the shrimp in the tortillas and serve with the Salsa Cruda.

Makes 6 to 8 servings

Salsa Cruda for Fish and Poultry, page 25

2^1/$_2$ to 3 pounds (12 to 15 per pound) shrimp, peeled and deveined

1 cup butter

3 to 4 tablespoons minced garlic

6 to 8 flour tortillas (6-inch)

Salt and freshly ground black pepper

Lime wedges

Shrimp Satay

Prep and cook time: About 1 hour

1 Prepare the Spice Paste: Trim and discard the tough top and root end of the lemon grass. Remove and discard the tough outer layers. Thinly slice the tender inner part, then pulse in a food processor until finely chopped. Add the shallots, garlic, red or green jalapeños, fresh galangal (if using), ginger, coriander seed, turmeric, and macadamia nuts, and process until finely ground. Heat the oil in an 8- to 10-inch frying pan over high heat and add the spice mixture. Stir until the paste is slightly dark and dry, 6 to 8 minutes. Set aside to use hot or cool.

2 Soak 24 wooden skewers in water to cover for 30 minutes. Prepare a grill for cooking over high heat. First, oil the grill rack. If using a charcoal grill, prepare a solid bed of hot coals. If using a gas grill, preheat to high (you can hold your hand 1 to 2 inches above grill level only 2 to 3 seconds).

3 Rinse the shrimp and pat dry. Mix the Spice Paste, tomato paste, and lemon juice, and coat the shrimp with the mixture.

4 Lay 2 or 3 shrimp flat, parallel to each other, and run 2 skewers about 1 inch apart through the center of the shrimp. Repeat to skewer the remaining shrimp.

5 Lay the shrimp on the grill rack. Close the lid if using a gas grill. Cook, turning occasionally, until shrimp are opaque but moist-looking in center of thickest part (cut to test), 5 to 6 minutes. Serve hot or at room temperature.

Makes 4 main-course or 8 first-course servings

....

Notes from The Sunset Grill

You can prepare the Spice Paste 3 days ahead. Cover and chill until ready to use or freeze to store it longer. If time is short, you can use 1/4 cup prepared Thai red curry paste instead. You can also coat the shrimp with the spice mixture and thread onto the skewers up to 1 day ahead. Wrap airtight and chill until it's time to grill.

1 1/2 pounds (21 to 25 per pound) shrimp, peeled and deveined

2 tablespoons fresh lemon juice

2 tablespoons tomato paste

SPICE PASTE

1 stalk fresh lemon grass

2 cups sliced shallots

3 tablespoons sliced garlic

1/2 cup sliced fresh red or green jalapeños

3 tablespoons sliced peeled fresh galangal (optional)

2 tablespoons thinly sliced peeled fresh ginger

1 1/2 teaspoons coriander seed

1 teaspoon ground dried turmeric

6 salted roasted macadamia nuts

2 tablespoons vegetable oil

Grilled Shrimp with Chile-Almond Sauce

Prep and cook time: About 1 hour

1 Prepare the Chile-Almond Sauce: In a bowl, soak the chile in 1 cup boiling water until soft, about 20 minutes, and drain. Preheat oven to 400°F. Slice the tomato in half lengthwise and remove the seeds. Drizzle about 1/2 teaspoon olive oil over the cut sides and sprinkle lightly with salt and pepper. Place the tomato halves on a baking sheet, cut side up, and bake until browned and soft, about 20 minutes. Heat 1 teaspoon olive oil in an 8- to 10-inch frying pan over medium heat. Add the garlic and stir often until lightly browned, about 5 minutes. In a food processor or blender, process the chile, tomato, garlic, red peppers, almonds, vinegar, and parsley until puréed. Add salt and pepper to taste. Pour the sauce into a bowl and set aside.

2 Prepare a grill for cooking over medium-high heat. First, oil the grill rack. If using a charcoal grill, prepare a solid bed of medium-hot coals. If using a gas grill, preheat to high and close the lid, then open the lid and lower the heat to medium-high (you can hold your hand 1 to 2 inches above grill level only 3 to 4 seconds).

3 Rinse the shrimp and pat dry. Thread the shrimp onto four 10- to 14-inch metal skewers. Brush with the olive oil and sprinkle with salt and pepper. Lay the shrimp on the grill rack. If using a gas grill, close the lid. Cook the shrimp, turning once, until opaque but still moist-looking in the center of thickest part (cut to test), 3 to 6 minutes total. Serve immediately with the Chile-Almond Sauce.

Makes 2 to 4 servings

....

Notes from The Sunset Grill

To toast the almonds, place in a baking pan and bake at 350°F, shaking the pan occasionally, until golden under skins, about 12 minutes. You can make the Chile-Almond Sauce up to 2 days ahead, then cover and chill until ready to use.

1 pound (26 to 30 per pound) shrimp, peeled and deveined

2 tablespoons olive oil

Salt and freshly ground black pepper

CHILE-ALMOND SAUCE

1 dried New Mexico or California chile, stemmed and seeded

1 Roma tomato (4 ounces), rinsed and cored

About 1 1/2 teaspoons olive oil

Salt and freshly ground black pepper

2 tablespoons sliced garlic

3/4 cup drained canned roasted red peppers

2 tablespoons toasted almonds (see Notes)

1 tablespoon sherry vinegar

1 tablespoon chopped flat-leaf parsley

Salt and freshly ground black pepper

Scallop Salad with Caribbean Flavors

Prep and cook time: About 45 minutes

1 Prepare a grill for cooking over high heat. First, oil the grill rack. If using a charcoal grill, prepare a solid bed of hot coals. If using a gas grill, preheat to high (you can hold your hand 1 to 2 inches above grill level only 2 to 3 seconds).

2 Rinse the scallops and dry with a paper towel. Sprinkle 1½ teaspoons fish rub evenly over the scallops and coat lightly with olive oil.

3 Lay the scallops on the grill rack. If using a gas grill, close the lid. Grill, turning once, until opaque throughout, about 3 minutes on each side. Remove the scallops to a plate and keep warm. Add the pineapple slices to the grill rack and grill, turning once, until golden brown and tender, about 3 minutes on each side. Remove the pineapple from the grill and chop it. Put the pineapple and its juice in a bowl.

4 Combine the salad greens, lettuce, pineapple, pineapple juice, avocado, and mango in a large bowl.

5 Combine the lime juice, 2 teaspoons olive oil, and remaining ½ teaspoon fish rub in a small bowl. Pour the dressing over the salad and toss gently to mix well. Season to taste with salt and freshly ground black pepper. Divide the salad evenly among 4 plates and top with 3 scallops each. Serve immediately.

Makes 4 servings

2 teaspoons extra-virgin olive oil, plus more for coating and grilling

12 large sea scallops (about 1½ pounds)

2 teaspoons fish rub (such as Spice Rub for Fish and Poultry, page 24)

5 slices (½-inch) fresh pineapple

4 cups mixed salad greens

4 cups torn Boston lettuce (about 2 small heads)

⅓ cup peeled and diced avocado

½ cup diced fresh mango

2 tablespoons fresh lime juice

Salt and freshly ground black pepper

Grilled Lobster with Anise Butter

Prep and cook time: About 45 minutes

1   Prepare a grill for cooking over high heat. First, oil the grill rack. If using a charcoal grill, prepare a solid bed of hot coals. If using a gas grill, preheat to high (you can hold your hand 1 to 2 inches above grill level only 2 to 3 seconds).

2   If using lobster tails, cut them in half lengthwise. If using live lobsters, cook them in boiling salted water for 2 minutes and drain. Cut the lobsters in half lengthwise and crack the claws with a nutcracker or hammer.

3   In a small saucepan, combine the butter, lemon juice, tarragon, ground anise seeds, salt, and pepper over medium-high heat and cook until the butter is melted. Brush the cut side of the lobsters with the flavored butter and arrange, cut side down, on the grill rack. If using a gas grill, close the lid. Cook until the cut sides are opaque and lightly grill-marked, about 6 minutes. Turn and cook, brushing the cut sides several times with the butter, until the flesh is opaque throughout, 3 to 5 minutes longer. Serve hot with the remaining anise butter for dipping.

Makes 4 servings

4 lobster tails, thawed if frozen, or 4 live Maine lobsters (1$1/4$ to 1$1/2$ pounds each)

$1/2$ cup unsalted butter

2 tablespoons fresh lemon juice

1 tablespoon chopped fresh tarragon or 1 teaspoon dried tarragon

1 teaspoon anise seeds, ground in a mortar or spice grinder

$1/2$ teaspoon salt

$1/4$ teaspoon freshly ground black pepper

Notes from The Sunset Grill
Anise seeds have a lovely, sweet licorice flavor that mixes well with melted butter and lemon juice. The anise butter is a wonderful complement to lightly grilled lobsters.

poultry

103

Grilled Chicken, Pear, and Spinach Salad

Prep and cook time: About 1½ hours

1 Prepare the Spice Crisps: Preheat the oven to 375°F. In a small bowl, mix the chili powder, coriander, and garlic salt. Split the pocket breads apart to make 8 rounds. Lay the rounds, rough side up, on two 12- by 15-inch baking sheets. Brush the tops lightly with vinegar, then sprinkle evenly with the spice mixture. Bake until the rounds are crisp and lightly browned, 8 to 10 minutes. Set aside.

2 Rinse the chicken and pat it dry. Trim off and discard any excess fat. Season to taste with salt and pepper.

3 Prepare a grill for cooking over high heat. First, oil the grill rack. If using a charcoal grill, prepare a solid bed of hot coals. If using a gas grill, preheat to high (you can hold your hand 1 to 2 inches above grill level only 2 to 3 seconds). Lay the chicken breasts on the grill rack. If using a gas grill, close the lid. Cook the chicken, turning once, until no longer pink in center of thickest part (cut to test), 7 to 9 minutes. Let cool.

4 In a 6- to 8-inch frying pan over medium heat, stir the almonds until golden, about 6 minutes. Let cool.

5 Cut the chicken into ¼-inch-thick strips 2 to 3 inches long. Rinse the pear and cut lengthwise into quarters. Trim the core from each quarter and discard. Thinly slice the quarters lengthwise.

6 In a large bowl, mix the balsamic vinegar, olive oil, and ½ teaspoon garlic salt. Add the spinach, green onions, almonds, chicken, and ¾ of the pear slices and mix gently. Season to taste with salt and pepper.

7 Divide the salad evenly among 4 dinner plates. Top each plate with the remaining pear slices and sprinkle with the cheese. Serve with the Spice Crisps.

Makes 4 servings

4 boned, skinned chicken breast halves

Salt

Freshly ground black pepper

⅓ cup slivered almonds

1 firm-ripe pear

½ cup balsamic vinegar

2 tablespoons extra-virgin olive oil

½ teaspoon garlic salt

¾ pound baby spinach leaves, rinsed and crisped

¼ cup thinly sliced green onions (including tops)

⅓ cup crumbled feta cheese

SPICE CRISPS

½ teaspoon chili powder

½ teaspoon ground coriander

½ teaspoon garlic salt

4 pocket breads (6-inch)

1 tablespoon white wine vinegar

Persian Chicken Skewers

Prep and cook time: About 1 hour, plus 30 minutes to chill

1 In a bowl, mix the chicken, bread crumbs, egg yolk, onion,
turmeric, and 1/4 teaspoon salt. Cover and chill at least
30 minutes or up to 1 day.

2 Divide the chicken mixture into 4 equal portions. Dipping your
hands frequently in water to keep the mixture from sticking,
pat each portion around a flat metal skewer to form a log 1 inch
thick and about 7 inches long. Set aside.

3 Prepare a grill for cooking over high heat. First, oil the grill
rack. If using a charcoal grill, prepare a solid bed of hot coals.
If using a gas grill, preheat to high (you can hold your hand 1 to
2 inches above grill level only 2 to 3 seconds). One skewer at a
time, lay the chicken on the grill rack and rotate quickly to firm up
the surface of the meat. If using a gas grill, close the lid. Rotate the
skewers every 2 to 3 minutes until the meat is lightly browned and
firm at the skewer (cut to test), about 10 minutes total.

4 Cut or push the meat off the skewers. Season to taste with salt
and serve immediately.

Makes 4 servings

....

Notes from The Sunset Grill
*You can serve this dish with basmati rice, grilled tomatoes, and a
spray of herbs—parsley, basil, tarragon, cilantro, and dill—if you like.*

---

1 pound ground chicken

6 tablespoons fine dried bread crumbs

1 egg yolk

2 tablespoons minced onion

1/2 teaspoon ground dried turmeric

About 1/4 teaspoon salt

Chicken Satay with Spicy Peanut Sauce

Prep and cook time: About 1¹/2 hours, plus at least 4 hours to marinate

1 Prepare the Spicy Peanut Sauce: In a food processor, pulse the peanuts, garlic, chile, galangal, and sugar until finely ground. In a 2- to 3-quart pan over high heat, combine the peanut mixture, coconut milk, and sweet soy sauce. Bring to a boil, stirring constantly. Reduce the heat and simmer, uncovered, stirring occasionally, until the sauce is slightly darker and thicker, about 15 minutes. Add the lime juice and salt to taste. Keep warm or at room temperature (see Notes).

2 Rinse the chicken breasts and pat dry. Slice them diagonally across the grain into ¹/4-inch-thick strips.

3 In a large resealable plastic bag, mix ¹/2 cup water and the soy sauce, ginger, rice vinegar, sugar, and chili paste. Add the chicken. Seal the bag and let marinate in the refrigerator at least 4 hours or overnight.

4 Match the number of wooden skewers to the number of chicken strips and soak the skewers in water to cover for 30 minutes. Meanwhile, prepare a grill for cooking over high heat. First, oil the grill rack. If using a charcoal grill, prepare a solid bed of hot coals. If using a gas grill, preheat to high (you can hold your hand 1 to 2 inches above grill level only 2 to 3 seconds).

5 Lift the chicken from the marinade and thread a skewer through each strip. Discard the marinade. Lay the skewers on the grill rack and close the lid if using a gas grill. Grill the chicken, turning once, until it is no longer pink in the center (cut to test), about 5 minutes. Serve immediately with the Spicy Peanut Sauce on the side.

Makes 4 main-course or 8 first-course servings

....

Notes from The Sunset Grill

The Spicy Peanut Sauce recipe makes 4¹/2 cups. You can make the sauce, cover, and chill up to 2 days. Reheat the sauce over low heat. If it has thickened or looks slightly curdled, stir in a little water.

1 pound boned, skinned chicken breasts

¹/2 cup soy sauce

2 tablespoons minced fresh ginger

1 tablespoon rice vinegar

1 tablespoon sugar

2 teaspoons Asian chili paste

SPICY PEANUT SAUCE

¹/2 pound salted roasted peanuts

3 cloves garlic, peeled

1 to 1¹/2 teaspoons chopped fresh Thai chile or 1 to 2 tablespoons chopped fresh serrano chiles

2 tablespoons sliced peeled fresh galangal or fresh ginger

¹/4 cup chopped palm sugar or firmly packed brown sugar

2 cans (14 ounces each) coconut milk

¹/4 cup sweet soy sauce *(kecap manis)* or 2 tablespoons each soy sauce and sugar

About 3 tablespoons fresh lime juice

About ¹/2 teaspoon salt

Grilled Chipotle-Chicken Quesadillas

Prep and cook time: About 45 minutes

1 Prepare the Pico de Gallo: In a bowl, mix the tomatoes, onion, jalapeño chiles, cilantro, lime juice, and garlic. Add salt to taste. Set aside.

2 Prepare a grill for cooking over medium heat. First, oil the grill rack. If using a charcoal grill, prepare a solid bed of medium coals. If using a gas grill, preheat to high and close the lid, then open the lid and lower the heat to medium (you can hold your hand 1 to 2 inches above grill level only 4 to 5 seconds).

3 Rinse the chicken breasts and pat dry, then brush with olive oil and season with salt and pepper. Lay the chicken on the grill rack. If using a gas grill, close the lid. Cook the chicken, turning once, until cooked through (cut to test), about 4 to 5 minutes on each side. Slice the cooked chicken breasts into 1/4-inch-thick slices. Keep the chicken warm and the grill hot.

4 In a small bowl, whisk together the chipotle chile, sour cream, mayonnaise, lime juice, and cilantro.

5 Spread 1 tablespoon of the chipotle-lime sauce on each of the tortillas. Divide the cheese and chicken slices evenly among 4 of the tortillas. Top the cheese and chicken with the remaining tortillas, sauce side down.

6 Put the quesadillas onto the grill over medium heat. Grill, uncovered, turning once, until the cheese is melted and both sides are golden, about 2 minutes per side.

7 Slice each quesadilla into wedges and serve immediately with the Pico de Gallo on the side.

Makes 4 servings

4 boned, skinned chicken breast halves

1 tablespoon olive oil

Salt and freshly ground black pepper

1 canned chipotle chile in adobo sauce, drained and minced

1/4 cup sour cream

1/4 cup mayonnaise

1 tablespoon fresh lime juice

1 tablespoon chopped fresh cilantro

8 corn tortillas (6-inch)

2 cups grated Monterey jack cheese

PICO DE GALLO

2 cups diced tomatoes

1/2 cup diced onion

2 tablespoons minced jalapeño chiles

1/4 cup minced fresh cilantro

2 tablespoons fresh lime juice

1 teaspoon minced garlic

Salt to taste

Grilled Chicken Sandwiches with Fig Relish

Prep and cook time: About 1 hour

1 Prepare the Fig Relish: In a bowl, combine the vinegar, shallot, and salt. Let stand 10 minutes. Rinse the figs, pat dry, and trim off and discard the stem ends. Cut the figs into 1/2-inch chunks and add to the vinegar mixture. Stir in the mint and rosemary, breaking up the figs slightly with the spoon. Set aside.

2 Rinse the chicken and pat dry. Place each chicken breast half between 2 sheets of plastic wrap. With a flat mallet or rolling pin, gently pound to 1/2 inch thick. Brush both sides of the chicken lightly with olive oil and season with salt and pepper.

3 Prepare a grill for cooking over high heat. First, oil the grill rack. If using a charcoal grill, prepare a solid bed of hot coals. If using a gas grill, preheat to high (you can hold your hand 1 to 2 inches above grill level only 2 to 3 seconds).

4 Lay the chicken on the grill rack. If using a gas grill, close the lid. Cook, turning once, until the chicken is no longer pink in the center (cut to test), 3 to 4 minutes on each side. Meanwhile, brush both sides of the bread lightly with olive oil. When you turn the chicken, lay the bread slices on the grill and cook, turning once, until lightly toasted, about 2 minutes on each side.

5 To assemble each sandwich, top one slice of bread with about 1/4 cup arugula leaves. Place the chicken on the arugula and top with about 1/3 cup Fig Relish. Top with a second slice of grilled bread and serve immediately.

Makes 3 sandwiches

....

Notes from The Sunset Grill
The Fig Relish recipe makes 1 cup and is also good served with crackers or toasted baguette slices as a first course.

3 boned, skinned chicken breast halves (about 6 ounces each)

About 1/4 cup olive oil

Salt and freshly ground black pepper

6 slices sourdough bread

3/4 cup arugula leaves or salad mix, rinsed and crisped

FIG RELISH

1 1/2 tablespoons balsamic vinegar

1 tablespoon minced shallot

1/8 teaspoon salt

8 ounces ripe Mission figs

2 teaspoons chopped fresh mint leaves

1/4 teaspoon minced fresh rosemary leaves

Grilled Fusion Chicken

Prep and cook time: About 1 hour

1 Rinse the chicken breasts and pat dry. Place each chicken breast half between 2 sheets of plastic wrap. With a flat mallet or rolling pin, gently pound to 1/4 inch thick. In a shallow dish, whisk together the oil, tequila, lime juice, hot sauce, Worcestershire sauce, ginger, chile, and salt. Remove 1/3 cup of the marinade and set aside. Put the chicken in the remaining marinade, turn to coat, and let stand 30 minutes.

2 Prepare a grill for cooking over medium heat. First, oil the grill rack. If using a charcoal grill, prepare a solid bed of medium coals. If using a gas grill, preheat to high and close the lid, then open the lid and lower the heat to medium (you can hold your hand 1 to 2 inches above grill level only 4 to 5 seconds).

3 Lay the chicken on the grill rack. If using a gas grill, close the lid. Grill the chicken, turning once, until cooked through (cut to test), 3 to 4 minutes on each side.

4 In a small saucepan over medium-high heat, simmer the reserved marinade until reduced to 1/4 cup, about 2 minutes. Whisk in the cream, then remove from the heat. Drizzle the sauce over the chicken and garnish with cilantro if you like. Serve immediately.

Makes 4 servings

....

Notes from The Sunset Grill

You can substitute 1/2 cup extra-virgin olive oil mixed with 2 teaspoons minced garlic for the garlic-infused olive oil.

4 boned, skinned chicken breast halves

1/2 cup garlic-infused olive oil (see Notes)

2 tablespoons tequila

2 tablespoons fresh lime juice

1 1/2 teaspoons hot sauce

1 teaspoon Worcestershire sauce

1 teaspoon grated fresh ginger

1 teaspoon ground dried chipotle chile

1 teaspoon salt

1/3 cup heavy cream

Chopped fresh cilantro (optional)

Grilled Chicken with Lime and Pepper

Prep and cook time: About 30 minutes, plus 30 minutes to marinate

1 Combine the lime juice, sugar, pepper, oil, salt, and 1/4 cup water in a large bowl or resealable plastic bag. Stir to dissolve the sugar and salt. Set aside.

2 Rinse the chicken and pat dry. On a flat surface, lay 1 chicken breast half between 2 large pieces of plastic wrap. Using a mallet or a small saucepan, pound the chicken to 1/4 to 1/3 inch thick. Put the chicken in the bowl or plastic bag with the marinade. Repeat with the remaining breasts halves. Cover the bowl or seal the bag and let the chicken marinate in the refrigerator 30 minutes.

3 Prepare a grill for cooking over medium-high heat. First, oil the grill rack. If using a charcoal grill, prepare a solid bed of medium-hot coals. If using a gas grill, preheat to high and close the lid, then open the lid and lower the heat to medium-high (you can hold your hand 1 to 2 inches above grill level only 3 to 4 seconds).

4 Remove the chicken from the marinade and lay on the grill rack. If using a gas grill, close the lid. Grill the chicken, turning once, until cooked through (cut to test), about 4 minutes on each side. Serve immediately.

Makes 4 servings

1/2 cup lime juice (from about 4 limes)

3 tablespoons sugar

2 tablespoons freshly ground black pepper

1 tablespoon olive oil

1 teaspoon salt

4 boned, skinned chicken breast halves

....

Notes from The Sunset Grill
You can grill vegetables and thick corn tortillas to serve alongside.

Tamil Chicken Wings
with Cucumber Salad

Prep and cook time: About 35 minutes, plus at least 1 hour to marinate

1 Remove the stem end and tough outer leaves from the lemon grass. Cut the inner stalk into chunks and put in a food processor with the cilantro, garlic, salt, turmeric, and pepper. Process until finely minced. Pat the mixture over the chicken wings. Cover and chill at least 1 hour or up to 1 day.

2 Prepare a grill for cooking over medium heat. First, oil the grill rack. If using a charcoal grill, prepare a solid bed of medium coals. If using a gas grill, preheat to high and close the lid, then open the lid and lower the heat to medium (you can hold your hand 1 to 2 inches above grill level only 4 to 5 seconds).

3 Remove the chicken wings from the marinade and lay them on the grill rack. If using a gas grill, close the lid. Cook the chicken, turning occasionally, until no longer pink at the bone (cut to test), about 15 minutes total.

4 Meanwhile, prepare the Cucumber Salad: In a bowl, combine the cucumber, onion, chile, yogurt, and lime juice. Season to taste with salt.

5 Transfer the cooked chicken wings to a platter and serve with the Cucumber Salad alongside.

Makes 4 servings

1 stalk (about 2 ounces) fresh lemon grass or 3 large strips fresh lemon zest (yellow part only), chopped

3/4 cup fresh cilantro sprigs, rinsed

8 cloves garlic, peeled

1 teaspoon salt

1 teaspoon ground turmeric

1/2 teaspoon white or black pepper

8 chicken wings (about 1 3/4 pounds total)

CUCUMBER SALAD

1 cucumber (about 12 ounces), peeled and thinly sliced

1/4 cup thinly sliced red onion

1 fresh jalapeño chile (about 1/2 ounce), stemmed, seeded, and thinly sliced

2 tablespoons plain yogurt

1 tablespoon fresh lime juice

Salt to taste

Notes from The Sunset Grill

Grilled Green-Onion Breads, page 68, make a great accompaniment to this dish.

Sticky Coconut Chicken

Prep and cook time: About 1 hour, plus 1 hour to marinate

1 Rinse the chicken and pat dry. In a large bowl, mix the coconut milk, ginger, pepper, and red pepper flakes. Add the chicken, and mix. Cover airtight and chill at least 1 hour or up to 1 day.

2 Prepare a grill for cooking over high heat. First, oil the grill rack. If using a charcoal grill, prepare a solid bed of hot coals. If using a gas grill, preheat to high (you can hold your hand 1 to 2 inches above grill level only 2 to 3 seconds).

3 Lift the chicken from the bowl. Transfer the marinade to a small saucepan, bring to a boil, and cook for 2 minutes. Pull the thighs open and lay them flat, skin side down, on the grill rack. If using a gas grill, close the lid. Cook, turning once and basting frequently with the marinade, until the meat is no longer pink in the center of the thickest part (cut to test), about 6 minutes on each side.

4 Meanwhile, prepare the Glaze: In a 2- to 3-quart pan, combine the rice vinegar, sugar, soy sauce, and red pepper flakes. Bring to a boil over high heat and cook until the mixture is reduced to $^{1}/_{2}$ cup, 8 to 10 minutes.

5 Transfer the thighs to a warm platter and pour the Glaze over the meat. Garnish the platter with the green onions and serve immediately.

Makes 6 to 8 servings

6 to 8 boned, skinned chicken thighs (1$^{1}/_{4}$ to 1$^{1}/_{2}$ pounds total)

$^{3}/_{4}$ cup canned coconut milk (stir before measuring)

1 tablespoon minced fresh ginger

1 teaspoon freshly ground black pepper

1 teaspoon red pepper flakes

4 or 5 green onions, ends trimmed, cut lengthwise into thin slivers (including tops)

GLAZE

$^{3}/_{4}$ cup rice vinegar

$^{1}/_{2}$ cup sugar

3 tablespoons soy sauce

1 teaspoon red pepper flakes

Grilled Chicken with Sweet Onions and Peppers

Prep and cook time: About 1¹/₂ hours

1   In a large pan over medium heat, warm the olive oil. Add the onions and peppers, cover, and cook, stirring occasionally, until very juicy and almost tender, about 20 minutes. Add the port, capers, and thyme, and stir often, uncovered, until all the liquid has evaporated and the vegetables are very tender and beginning to brown, about 30 minutes longer. Remove from the heat. Season with salt and pepper to taste.

2   In an 8- to 10-quart pan over high heat, bring about 3 quarts water to a boil. Rinse the chicken, remove any excess fat, and immerse in the boiling water. Return the water to a boil, then cover, reduce the heat, and simmer until the meat is no longer pink in the center of the thickest part (cut to test), about 15 minutes. Lift the chicken from the water, drain, and pat dry.

3   Prepare a grill for cooking over medium-high heat. First, oil the grill rack. If using a charcoal grill, prepare a solid bed of medium-hot coals. If using a gas grill, preheat to high and close the lid, then open the lid and lower the heat to medium-high (you can hold your hand 1 to 2 inches above grill level only 3 to 4 seconds).

4   Season both sides of the chicken with salt and pepper. Lay the thighs, skin side down, on the grill rack. If using a gas grill, close the lid. Cook the chicken, turning once, until nicely browned, about 4 minutes on each side.

5   Transfer the chicken to a platter. Spoon the onion-pepper mixture over the chicken, sprinkle with parsley, and serve immediately.

Makes 6 servings

¹/₄ **cup extra-virgin olive oil**

2 red onions, thinly slivered lengthwise

1¹/₂ **pounds sweet peppers (such as red bell or Gypsy), stemmed, seeded, and slivered lengthwise**

¹/₂ **cup ruby port**

¹/₃ **cup drained capers**

3 tablespoons chopped fresh thyme leaves

Salt and freshly ground black pepper

12 chicken thighs (6 to 8 ounces each)

¹/₄ **cup chopped flat-leaf parsley**

Barbecued Chicken with Asian Flavors

Prep and cook time: About 1 hour, plus 4 hours to marinate

1 Rinse the chicken and pat dry. Combine the brown sugar, soy sauce, lime juice, red pepper, curry powder, and garlic in a large resealable plastic bag and add the chicken. Seal and marinate in the refrigerator at least 4 hours or overnight, turning occasionally.

2 Prepare a grill for cooking over medium-high heat. First, oil the grill rack. If using a charcoal grill, prepare a solid bed of medium-hot coals. If using a gas grill, preheat to high and close the lid, then open the lid and lower the heat to medium-high (you can hold your hand 1 to 2 inches above grill level only 3 to 4 seconds).

3 Remove the chicken from the bag. Transfer the marinade to a small saucepan, bring to a boil, and cook for 2 minutes.

4 Lay the chicken on the grill rack. If using a gas grill, close the lid. Grill the chicken, turning once and basting frequently with the marinade, until the meat is no longer pink in the center of the thickest part (cut to test), about 8 minutes on each side. Garnish with the lime wedges and green onion tops if you like, and serve immediately.

4 servings

8 skinned chicken thighs (6 ounces each)

1/4 cup firmly packed brown sugar

1/4 cup soy sauce

1 tablespoon fresh lime juice

1/2 teaspoon crushed red pepper

1/4 teaspoon curry powder

3 cloves garlic, minced

Lime wedges (optional)

Green onion tops (optional)

Soy Sauce
Savory, salty, and strongly flavored, soy sauce is made by fermenting soybeans with roasted grains. It is a key flavor in many Asian cuisines and contributes a distinctive deep taste to marinades. For the best flavor, look for naturally fermented sauce, widely available in supermarkets.

Paella Valanciana

Prep and cook time: About 2½ hours

1 Pour the lima beans into a colander. Sort and remove debris, then rinse and drain the beans. In a 4- to 5-quart pan over high heat, bring 2½ to 3 quarts water and the beans to a boil and cook for 2 minutes. Cover tightly, remove from heat, and let stand for 1 hour. Drain the beans, reserving 2 quarts of the cooking liquid. Keep the cooking liquid hot.

2 Rinse the chicken and pat dry. Cut each thigh in half lengthwise along one side of the bone. Pull off and discard any lumps of fat. Rinse the green beans, remove and discard the stem ends and any tough strings, and cut the beans into 3-inch lengths.

3 If using a charcoal grill (at least 22 inches wide), ignite 160 briquets (about 9½ pounds) on the firegrate, and open dampers. When coals are dotted with ash, 20 to 30 minutes, spread into an even double layer about 2 inches wider than the base of the paella pan. Set the grill 4 to 6 inches above the charcoal. Let the coals burn down until they're hot (you can hold your hand 1 to 2 inches above grill level only 2 to 3 seconds), 5 to 10 minutes. If using a gas grill (at least 19 inches wide), turn the temperature to high, close the lid, and let heat for 10 minutes.

4 Set a 17-inch paella pan on the grill over the hot coals or high heat on the gas grill. Add 2 tablespoons olive oil to the pan and spread with a metal spatula to coat the bottom of the pan. When the oil is hot, add the chicken pieces (close lid on gas grill). Cook, turning once, until lightly browned, about 4 minutes on each side.

5 Add the tomatoes and stir until most of the juices have evaporated, 1 to 2 minutes. Stir in the remaining 1 tablespoon oil, the green beans, 1½ teaspoons salt, paprika, and turmeric. Add the soaked lima beans and the reserved 2 quarts hot cooking liquid. Make note of the level of liquid in the pan—the distance from the pan rim or handle rivets to the level of the liquid. (Close lid on gas grill.) Bring to a gentle boil.

6 Boil gently to flavor broth, 25 to 30 minutes (on gas grill, regulate heat as needed to maintain a gentle boil). Remove about 1 cup broth from the pan. Add enough water to match the

1 cup large dried lima beans (6 ounces)

3 pounds bone-in chicken thighs

1 pound fresh Italian (Romano) or regular green beans, or thawed frozen Italian green beans

3 tablespoons olive oil

1 cup canned diced tomatoes

About 1½ teaspoons salt

½ teaspoon paprika

½ teaspoon dried turmeric

2½ cups medium-grain white rice

2 lemons, cut into wedges

original level of the liquid, 3 to 5 cups. Taste the broth in the pan and season to taste with more salt. Also taste the reserved broth and season with salt.

7 Pour the rice in a strip down the center of the pan. Draw the spoon or spatula in a wide zigzag pattern through the rice and across the pan to distribute the rice evenly. Push any grains floating above the broth back under. Simmer, without stirring, until the rice is tender to bite, 25 to 30 minutes. If the rice begins to scorch before it is tender, remove the pan from the heat and let the coals burn down to a lower temperature before continuing. (On gas grill, close the lid and regulate the heat so the liquid simmers briskly in the beginning, then lower the heat when most of the liquid has evaporated. Rotate the pan occasionally so the bottom cooks evenly.) If the rice is still firm, drizzle about 1/2 cup of the reserved broth evenly over the top and cook for a few minutes more. Repeat if necessary.

8 With the spoon or spatula, push aside a little of the top layer of rice to see if there is a brown crust on the bottom. If one hasn't formed yet, cook a few minutes more (adjust the gas heat as necessary to brown, but not burn, the rice). Remove the paella from the heat and let stand for about 5 minutes. Season to taste with salt. Serve immediately with the lemon wedges alongside.

Makes 8 to 10 servings

Notes from The Sunset Grill

If using a gas grill, make sure the paella pan fits. If using charcoal, make sure the ingredients are ready before you start the fire so you don't miss the peak heat. Follow the steps carefully, and the charcoal fire should cool down gradually as needed.

Tasty Grilled Chicken

Prep and cook time: About 1½ hours, plus 2 hours to marinate

1. Rinse the chicken and pat dry. Combine the orange juice, lemon juice, soy sauce, sherry, garlic, vinegar, basil oil, onion powder, sesame oil, salt, and hot pepper sauce in a large resealable plastic bag. Add the chicken to the bag and seal. Marinate in the refrigerator at least 2 hours or overnight, turning the bag occasionally.

2. Prepare a grill for cooking over medium-high heat. First, oil the grill rack. If using a charcoal grill, prepare a solid bed of medium-hot coals. If using a gas grill, preheat to high and close the lid, then open the lid and lower the heat to medium-high (you can hold your hand 1 to 2 inches above grill level only 3 to 4 seconds).

3. Remove the chicken from the bag. Transfer the marinade to a small saucepan, bring to a boil, and cook for 2 minutes.

4. Lay the chicken on the grill rack. If using a gas grill, close the lid. Grill, turning and basting frequently with the marinade, until the chicken is cooked through (cut to test), about 30 minutes. Garnish with green onion strips if you like, and serve immediately.

Makes 4 servings

8 skinned chicken drumsticks (about 2¼ pounds)

1 cup fresh orange juice

2 tablespoons fresh lemon juice

4 teaspoons soy sauce

1 tablespoon dry sherry

1½ teaspoons bottled minced garlic

1½ teaspoons balsamic vinegar

1½ teaspoons basil oil or olive oil

1 teaspoon onion powder

1 teaspoon dark sesame oil

½ teaspoon salt

¼ teaspoon hot pepper sauce

Green onion strips (optional)

Oranges

In season throughout the winter months but available year-round, fresh oranges add bright sweet-tangy flavor to marinades. The Valencia variety is excellent for juicing; widely available navels work well, too. For the best juice yield, choose smooth-skinned oranges that are heavy for their size.

Chicken Piri-Piri

Prep and cook time: About 1 1/2 hours, plus at least 4 hours to marinate

1   Prepare the Piri-Piri Marinade: Mix the lemon juice, olive oil, garlic, red pepper flakes, oregano, thyme, cumin, and salt in a bowl.

2   Rinse the chicken and pat dry. Trim off and discard excess fat and put the chicken in a large bowl. Stir the Piri-Piri Marinade, then pour it over the chicken, turning the pieces to coat. Cover and chill at least 4 hours or overnight, turning the chicken occasionally.

3   Prepare a grill for cooking over medium heat. First, oil the grill rack. If using a charcoal grill, prepare a solid bed of medium coals. If using a gas grill, preheat to high and close the lid, then open the lid and lower the heat to medium (you can hold your hand 1 to 2 inches above grill level only 4 to 5 seconds).

4   With tongs, lift the chicken from the marinade and drain well. Lay the chicken on the grill rack. If using a gas grill, close the lid. Cook, turning occasionally, until the skin is well browned and no longer pink at the bone (cut to test), about 40 minutes total. Brush occasionally with the marinade until about 10 minutes before the chicken is done. Transfer the cooked chicken to a platter and cover loosely with foil to keep warm.

5   Pour the remaining marinade into a 1 1/2- to 2-quart pan over medium-high heat. Bring the mixture to a boil, reduce the heat and simmer, stirring occasionally, about 2 minutes. Add the butter and stir until melted and incorporated. Remove the sauce from the heat and keep warm until ready to serve.

6   Garnish the chicken with the lemon wedges and serve with the piri-piri sauce alongside.

Makes 6 to 8 servings

....

Notes from The Sunset Grill
Piri-piri is a fiery sauce for grilled foods, with roots tracing back to the former Portuguese colony of Mozambique.

2 chickens (3 1/2 to 4 pounds each), each cut into 8 pieces

1/2 cup butter

Lemon wedges

PIRI-PIRI MARINADE

1 cup fresh lemon juice

3/4 cup olive oil

1/4 cup minced garlic

2 tablespoons red pepper flakes

2 teaspoons dried oregano

1 teaspoon dried thyme

1 teaspoon ground cumin

1 teaspoon salt

Wine-Brined Grilled Chicken

Prep and cook time: About 1 hour, plus 24 hours to soak in brine

1 Rinse the chicken and pat dry. Trim off any excess fat. In a large, deep roasting pan, add the wine, shallots, tarragon, salt, and sugar, and stir until the salt and sugar are dissolved. Add the chicken quarters and turn to coat. Cover and let brine in the refrigerator for 24 hours, turning once.

2 Lift the chicken from the brine and discard the brine. Pat the chicken dry.

3 Prepare a grill for cooking over medium-high heat. First, oil the grill rack. If using a charcoal grill, prepare a solid bed of medium-hot coals. If using a gas grill, preheat to high and close the lid, then open the lid and lower the heat to medium-high (you can hold your hand 1 to 2 inches above grill level only 3 to 4 seconds).

4 Lay the chicken quarters on the grill rack. If using a gas grill, close the lid. Cook, turning frequently, until browned on both sides and no longer pink at the bone (cut to test), about 25 minutes. Pile the quarters on a platter and serve immediately.

Makes 8 servings

....

Notes from The Sunset Grill

Have your butcher remove the backs from the chickens and quarter the birds. To mince such a large quantity of shallots, use a food processor.

2 chickens (about 3^1/$_2$ pounds each), necks and giblets removed, cut into quarters (see Notes)

1 bottle (750 milliliters) Sauvignon Blanc or other dry white wine

2 cups minced shallots (see Notes)

1 cup chopped fresh tarragon

^{1}/$_4$ cup kosher salt

2 tablespoons sugar

Smoke-Roasted Chicken

Prep and cook time: About 1³/₄ hours

1   In a medium bowl, cover the wood chips in water to soak at least 30 minutes. Drain just before using.

2   Meanwhile, prepare a grill for cooking over indirect heat. First, oil the grill rack. If using a charcoal grill, light about 60 briquets and let burn until covered with ash, 20 to 30 minutes, then mound them to one side. Place a drip pan on the side cleared of coals—this is the indirect-heat area. If using a gas grill, turn all burners to high and close the lid. When the temperature inside the grill reaches 350° to 400°F, lift the lid, turn off one of the burners, and lower the other burner(s) to medium. Place a drip pan under the turned-off burner—this is the indirect-heat area.

3   While the grill is heating, in a food processor, combine the garlic, chili powder, thyme, rosemary, olive oil, salt, and pepper. Process until the mixture forms a paste.

4   Rinse the chicken inside and out and pat dry. Press down on the breastbone of the chicken to flatten the bird slightly. Rub the paste evenly all over the chicken.

5   If using a charcoal grill, scatter half of the wood chips over the coals. If using a gas grill, place all the wood chips in the metal smoking box or in a foil pan directly on the heat in a corner. Set the oiled grill rack in place.

6   Place the chicken over the drip pan, breast side down. Cover the grill. If using a charcoal grill, adjust the vents so that they're open halfway. Cook 40 minutes, then turn the chicken over. If using charcoal, scatter another 20 briquets over the coals, along with the remaining wood chips. Cover the barbecue again.

7   Continue cooking the chicken until the thigh meat is no longer pink (cut to test) and a thermometer inserted in thickest part of the breast reaches 170°F, about 40 minutes longer. Transfer the chicken to a board or platter, cover loosely with foil, and let rest 10 minutes before serving.

Makes 6 servings

1 cup (about 3 ounces) hickory, mesquite, or applewood chips

12 cloves garlic, peeled

1 tablespoon chili powder

¹/₃ cup chopped fresh thyme leaves

¹/₃ cup chopped fresh rosemary leaves

¹/₄ cup olive oil

1 tablespoon salt

1 tablespoon freshly ground black pepper

1 chicken (4 to 5 pounds)

Brick-Grilled Cornish Hens

Prep and cook time: About 1½ hours, plus at least 30 minutes to marinate

1 Remove the giblets from the hens if present, and discard. Pull off and discard any lumps of fat. With poultry shears or kitchen scissors, cut along one side of each backbone. Then cut along the other side of each backbone and remove it. Discard the backbones. Rinse the hens well and pat dry. Pull the hens open and set skin side up on a flat surface. With your hand, press to flatten.

2 In a 9- by 13-inch baking dish, mix the lemon juice, parsley, olive oil, garlic, basil, oregano, pepper, red pepper flakes, and ½ teaspoon salt. Place the hens in the dish and rub the mixture all over them. Cover and chill at least 30 minutes or overnight.

3 Prepare a grill for cooking over medium heat. First, oil the grill rack. If using a charcoal grill, prepare a solid bed of medium coals. If using a gas grill, preheat to high and close the lid, then open the lid and lower the heat to medium (you can hold your hand 1 to 2 inches above grill level only 4 to 5 seconds).

4 Set the hens, skin side down and side by side, on a 12- by 17-inch section of the grill rack. If using a gas grill, close the lid. Set a 12- by 17-inch roasting pan, right side up, on the hens. Distribute 4 clean bricks (5 to 6 pounds each) evenly in the pan.

5 Cover the grill (open vents for charcoal) and cook until the skin is well browned (lift the pan to check), about 15 minutes. Remove the weighted pan and, with a wide spatula, turn the birds over. Cover the grill and cook without the weighted pan until the thigh meat is no longer pink (cut to test), 5 to 10 minutes longer.

6 Transfer the hens, skin side up, to a platter. With a knife or poultry shears, cut the hens into halves if you like. Serve with lemon wedges to squeeze over the hens and salt to taste.

Makes 4 servings

....

Notes from The Sunset Grill
This grilling method works well for chicken, too.

4 Cornish hens (about 1¾ pounds each)

¼ cup fresh lemon juice

¼ cup chopped parsley

About 3 tablespoons olive oil

3 tablespoons minced garlic

1 teaspoon dried basil

1 teaspoon dried oregano

½ teaspoon coarsely ground black pepper

½ teaspoon red pepper flakes

About ½ teaspoon salt

Lemon wedges

Grilled Duck with Mushrooms and Asparagus

Prep and cook time: About 1 hour, plus 24 hours to marinate

1 Rinse the duck and pat dry. Combine the rosemary, parsley, 1 tablespoon olive oil, and garlic in a large resealable plastic bag. Add the duck, seal the bag, and marinate in the refrigerator overnight or up to 2 days.

2 Prepare a grill for cooking over medium-high heat. First, oil the grill rack. If using a charcoal grill, prepare a solid bed of medium-hot coals. If using a gas grill, preheat to high and close the lid, then open the lid and lower the heat to medium-high (you can hold your hand 1 to 2 inches above grill level only 3 to 4 seconds).

3 Remove the duck from the bag and season with 1/4 teaspoon salt and 1/8 teaspoon pepper. Place the duck breasts on the grill rack. If using a gas grill, close the lid. Grill, turning once, until just barely pink in the center, about 4 minutes on each side. It is important not to overcook the duck. Remove the duck from the grill, cover, and let stand 10 minutes.

4 While duck stands, heat 3 tablespoons olive oil in a large nonstick skillet over medium-high heat. Add the mushrooms, 1/8 teaspoon salt, and the remaining 1/8 teaspoon pepper, and sauté until tender, about 10 minutes. Add the asparagus and sauté until crisp-tender, about 4 minutes more.

5 Whisk together the remaining 1/8 teaspoon salt, vinegar, and truffle oil. Divide the mushroom mixture evenly among 4 dinner plates. Cut the duck across the grain into thin slices. Top the mushrooms on each plate with duck slices and drizzle with the vinaigrette. Serve immediately.

Makes 4 servings

4 boned, skinned duck breast halves (6 ounces each)

2 tablespoons chopped fresh rosemary

2 tablespoons chopped fresh parsley

About 4 tablespoons olive oil

3 cloves garlic, minced

1/2 teaspoon salt

1/4 teaspoon freshly ground black pepper

3 cups thinly sliced shiitake mushroom caps (about 5 ounces)

2 cups thinly sliced cremini mushroom caps (about 5 ounces)

1/4 pound asparagus, trimmed and cut into pieces

11/2 tablespoons Champagne vinegar

11/2 teaspoons truffle oil

Grilled Turkey with Thai Flavors

Prep and cook time: About 2 hours

1 Rinse the turkey thighs and pat dry. In a bowl, mix the basil, cilantro, mint, garlic, olive oil, brown sugar, soy sauce, ginger, fish sauce, chili paste, and salt. Spread about 2 tablespoons of the mixture evenly over the boned side of 1 turkey thigh. Set the remaining thigh, boned side down, over the herb mixture, aligning it with the first thigh. Tie the thighs together at 1-inch intervals with kitchen string to make a cylinder about 3 inches wide and 7 inches long. With your hands, pat the remaining herb mixture evenly all over the roast.

2 Prepare a grill for cooking over indirect heat. First, oil the grill rack. If using a charcoal grill, light 60 briquets and let burn until covered with ash, 20 to 30 minutes, then push equal amounts to opposite sides. Add 5 more briquets to each mound of coals now and after 30 minutes. Place a drip pan in the center, away from the coals—this is the indirect-heat area. If using a gas grill, turn all burners to high and close the lid. When the temperature inside the grill reaches 350° to 400°F, lift the lid and turn off the center burner, leaving the others on high. Place a drip pan under the turned-off burner—this is the indirect-heat area.

3 Set the oiled grill rack in place and set the roast over the drip pan. Cover the barbecue (open vents for charcoal). Cook the roast until a thermometer inserted in center reaches 170°F, about 45 minutes.

4 Transfer the roast to a cutting board, cover loosely with foil, and let stand for 5 minutes. Remove the kitchen string and cut the roast into 1/2-inch-thick slices. Lay the slices on a platter, garnish with lime wedges, and serve immediately.

Makes 4 to 6 servings

....

Notes from The Sunset Grill
Have your butcher skin and bone the turkey thighs for you if need be.

2 skinned and boned turkey thighs (about 3/4 pounds each; see Notes)

1/4 cup chopped fresh basil leaves

1/4 cup chopped fresh cilantro

1/4 cup chopped fresh mint leaves

3 cloves garlic, minced

3 tablespoons olive oil

1 tablespoon firmly packed brown sugar

1 tablespoon soy sauce

2 teaspoons minced fresh ginger

2 teaspoons Asian fish sauce (*nuoc mam* or *nam pla*)

1/2 teaspoon Asian chili paste

1/2 teaspoon salt

Lime wedges for serving

pork, beef & lamb

Grilled Beer-Cooked Bratwursts

Prep and cook time: About 40 minutes

1 Bring the beer to a boil in a large, wide pot. Add the bratwursts and onion and simmer 15 minutes. Cover, remove from heat, and let stand until ready to grill.

2 Prepare a grill for cooking over medium heat. First, oil the grill rack. If using a charcoal grill, prepare a solid bed of medium coals. If using a gas grill, preheat to high and close the lid, then open the lid and lower the heat to medium (you can hold your hand 1 to 2 inches above grill level only 4 to 5 seconds). Using tongs or a slotted spoon, transfer the bratwursts to the grill rack. If using a gas grill, close the lid. Cook the bratwursts, turning once, until browned on both sides, about 8 minutes.

3 Meanwhile, drain the onions and set aside. Serve the bratwursts hot or warm, with the onions on the side.

Makes 12 servings

6 bottles (12 ounces each) medium-to heavy-bodied ale

12 bratwursts

1 large onion, halved lengthwise and sliced

....

Notes from The Sunset Grill

You can cook up to 8 more sausages without increasing the amount of beer or onion. These brats are delicious smeared with coarse-grain mustard and sandwiched on crusty rolls.

Barbecued Ribs with Chili Powder, Garlic, and Cumin

Prep and cook time: About 1½ hours, plus at least 8 hours to season

1. In a bowl, mix the chili powder, garlic powder, cumin, oregano, thyme, mustard, salt, pepper, and cloves. Rinse the ribs and pat dry. Rub the ribs all over with the spice mixture. Wrap airtight and chill 8 hours or overnight to season the ribs.

2. Prepare a grill for cooking over indirect heat. First, oil the grill rack. If using a charcoal grill, light 50 to 60 briquets and let burn until covered with ash, about 20 to 30 minutes, then mound them to one side. Place a drip pan on the side cleared of coals—this is the indirect-heat area. If using a gas grill, turn all burners to high and close the lid. When the temperature inside the grill reaches 350° to 400°F, lift the lid, turn off one of the burners, and lower the other burner(s) to medium. Place a drip pan under the turned-off burner—this is the indirect-heat area.

3. Set the oiled grill rack in place. Lay the ribs on the grill rack (not directly over heat) and cover the barbecue (if using charcoal, open vents). Cook until the meat is browned, about 15 minutes, turning the ribs once midway through the cooking time. Wrap the ribs in foil and return to the grill. Cook until the meat is tender when pierced, about 30 minutes longer.

4. Transfer the ribs to a platter and cut apart between the bones. Garnish with the lime wedges to squeeze over the ribs to taste.

Makes 4 main-course or 8 first-course servings

....

Notes from The Sunset Grill

Instead of just chili powder, equal parts of ground dried chipotle and ground dried pasilla chiles—both of which are available in well-stocked supermarkets or Latino markets—make an interesting blend. The ribs can be rubbed with the spice mixture up to 1 day ahead, then wrapped airtight and chilled.

¼ cup chili powder (see Notes)

1 tablespoon garlic powder

2 teaspoons ground cumin

1½ teaspoons dried oregano

1½ teaspoons dried thyme

¾ teaspoon hot dry mustard

¾ teaspoon salt

¼ teaspoon freshly ground black pepper

⅛ teaspoon ground cloves

1 rack baby back ribs (2¼ to 2½ pounds), fat trimmed, cut in half lengthwise

2 limes, quartered

Baby Back Ribs with Cherry-Zinfandel Sauce

Prep and cook time: About 2 hours

1 In a small bowl, mix the paprika, thyme, salt, and pepper. Rinse the ribs and pat dry. Rub the herb mixture over both sides of each rack. Wrap each rack in heavy-duty foil and set aside.

2 Prepare the Cherry-Zinfandel Sauce: Heat the olive oil in a medium saucepan over medium-high heat. Add the onion and garlic and cook, stirring, until soft, 8 minutes. Add the Zinfandel, ketchup, cherries, vinegar, Worcestershire sauce, brown sugar, mustard, ginger, pepper, anise seeds, and cayenne. Bring to a boil, reduce the heat and simmer, stirring, until the liquid begins to thicken slightly, 20 minutes. Let cool slightly. Pour the mixture into a blender, add 2 tablespoons lemon juice, and blend until smooth. Add more lemon juice to taste, and set the mixture aside.

3 Prepare a grill for cooking over indirect heat. First, oil the grill rack. If using a charcoal grill, light 50 to 60 briquets and let burn until covered with ash, about 20 to 30 minutes, then mound them to one side. Place a drip pan on the side cleared of coals. If using a gas grill, turn all burners to high and close the lid. When the temperature inside the grill reaches 400°F, lift the lid, turn off one of the burners, and lower the other burner(s) to medium. Place a drip pan under the turned-off burner.

4 Set the oiled grill rack in place. Lay the foil-wrapped ribs on the grill over the drip pan, meaty side up. Cover and cook until the ribs are tender when pierced (through the foil), 1 to 1¼ hours. Every 30 minutes of cooking, add 5 more briquets to the mound of coals. Carefully remove the foil from the ribs. Brush the meaty side of the ribs with the sauce, turn, and cook until browned, 10 minutes. Brush the bony sides, turn again, and cook until browned, about 10 minutes longer. Transfer the racks to a board and cut into individual ribs. Season to taste with salt and serve with the remaining sauce.

Makes 6 to 8 servings

¼ cup paprika

3 tablespoons dried thyme

1 tablespoon salt, plus more to taste

1½ tablespoons freshly ground black pepper

3 racks baby back ribs (7 to 8 pounds total)

CHERRY-ZINFANDEL SAUCE

1 tablespoon olive oil

1 onion, chopped

2 tablespoons chopped garlic

1½ cups dry red Zinfandel

1 cup ketchup

⅔ cup dried tart cherries

3 tablespoons cider vinegar

3 tablespoons Worcestershire sauce

3 tablespoons lightly packed light brown sugar

2 tablespoons Dijon mustard

2 tablespoons chopped fresh ginger

1 teaspoon freshly ground black pepper

1 teaspoon anise seeds

¼ teaspoon cayenne

About 3 tablespoons fresh lemon juice

Fijian-Style Barbecued Ribs

Prep and cook time: About 1 hour, plus at least 2 hours to marinate

1 Make the South Pacific Marinade: Pull off and discard the tough outer layers from the stalks of lemon grass. Trim and discard the stem ends and coarse tops. Cut the tender stalks into chunks. In a food processor or blender, combine the lemon grass and the remaining marinade ingredients. Purée until smooth and set aside.

2 Rinse the ribs and pat dry. Trim and discard any excess fat. If needed, cut the ribs into sections that will lie flat in a large roasting pan. Put the ribs and marinade in the pan and mix to coat. Cover and chill at least 2 hours or up to 1 day, turning the ribs occasionally.

3 Prepare a grill for cooking over indirect heat. First, oil the grill rack. If using a charcoal grill, light 50 to 60 briquets and let burn until covered with ash, about 20 to 30 minutes, then mound them to one side. Place a drip pan on the side cleared of coals—this is the indirect-heat area. If using a gas grill, turn all burners to high and close the lid. When the temperature inside the grill reaches 350° to 400°F, lift the lid, turn off one of the burners, and lower the other burner(s) to medium-high. Place a drip pan under the turned-off burner—this is the indirect-heat area.

4 Set the oiled grill rack in place. Lift the ribs from the pan and reserve the marinade. Lay the meat on the grill over the drip pan and cover the barbecue (open vents for charcoal). Turn the ribs as needed until well browned on each side, about 40 minutes total.

5 Meanwhile, toast the sesame seeds in a dry pan over medium-high heat, stirring frequently, until golden brown and fragrant, about 5 minutes. Remove from the heat and let cool. Bring the reserved marinade to a boil over high heat, stirring occasionally, for about 2 minutes. Season to taste with salt and pour into a bowl.

6 Transfer the ribs to a platter. Sprinkle with the cilantro and sesame seeds and serve with the sauce alongside.

Makes 6 to 8 servings

6 pounds baby back ribs

3 tablespoons sesame seeds

Salt

3 tablespoons chopped fresh cilantro

SOUTH PACIFIC MARINADE

2 stalks fresh lemon grass

1 can (14 ounces) coconut milk

1/2 cup coarsely chopped fresh cilantro

1/2 cup firmly packed brown sugar

1/3 cup soy sauce

1/4 cup coarsely chopped shallots

2 tablespoons chopped garlic

2 tablespoons chopped fresh ginger

2 tablespoons toasted sesame oil

2 tablespoons hoisin sauce

2 tablespoons Asian chili-garlic sauce

Chipotle Pork Roast

Prep and cook time: About 2½ hours, plus at least 4 hours to marinate

1 Rinse the pork and pat dry. Cut the garlic into ½-inch slices. Cut ½-inch slits all over the meat and insert the garlic slices in the slits. Season with salt and pepper. Place the meat in a 1-gallon heavy resealable plastic bag.

2 In a blender, purée the orange juice, chiles with sauce, oregano, and olive oil until smooth. Pour over the pork in the plastic bag, seal, and turn to coat. Set bag in a bowl. Chill at least 4 hours or up to 1 day, turning occasionally.

3 Prepare a grill for cooking over indirect heat. First, oil the grill rack. If using a charcoal grill, light 50 to 60 briquets and let burn until covered with ash, about 20 to 30 minutes, then mound them to one side. Place a drip pan on the side cleared of coals—this is the indirect-heat area. If using a gas grill, turn all burners to high and close the lid. When the temperature inside the grill reaches 350° to 400°F, lift the lid, turn off one of the burners, but keep the other burner(s) on high. Place a drip pan under the turned-off burner—this is the indirect-heat area.

4 Set the oiled grill rack in place. Lift the pork from the marinade and lay it on the grill over the drip pan. Cover the barbecue (open vents for charcoal). During the first hour, baste meat with the marinade occasionally. Every 30 minutes of cooking, add 5 more briquets to the mound of coals. Cook the pork until a thermometer inserted into the thickest part reaches 155°F, 1¼ to 1¾ hours. Discard the remaining marinade.

5 Transfer the pork to a platter, cover loosely with foil, and let rest about 10 minutes. Cut the meat into thin slices and squeeze juice from some of the orange wedges over the slices. Garnish the pork with the oregano sprigs and more orange wedges and serve immediately.

Makes 8 to 10 servings

1 boned center-cut pork loin (about 3 pounds), fat trimmed

10 cloves garlic, peeled

Salt and freshly ground black pepper

2 cups fresh orange juice

⅓ cup canned chipotle chiles, including sauce

1 tablespoon chopped fresh oregano leaves

1 tablespoon olive oil

Orange wedges

Oregano sprigs

Grilled Pork Tenderloin with Rosemary Pesto

Prep and cook time: About 2 hours

1   Toast the pine nuts in a dry skillet over medium-high heat, stirring frequently, until golden brown and fragrant, about 5 minutes. Remove from the heat and let cool.

2   Process the pine nuts, rosemary, mustard, and garlic in a food processor until smooth, stopping to scrape down sides. With the processor running, pour 1/4 cup of the olive oil through the food chute in a slow stream. Continue processing the mixture until smooth.

3   Place the tenderloins between 2 sheets of heavy-duty plastic wrap and flatten to 1/2 to 3/4 inch thick using a meat mallet or rolling pin. Spread the rosemary mixture evenly over the top of 2 of the tenderloins, then top with the remaining tenderloins and tie each stack together with kitchen string. Rub the remaining 1/4 cup of the olive oil over the pork, and season with salt and pepper.

4   Prepare a grill for cooking over indirect heat. First, oil the grill rack. If using a charcoal grill, light 50 to 60 briquets and let burn until covered with ash, about 20 to 30 minutes, then mound them to one side. Place a drip pan on the side cleared of coals—this is the indirect-heat area. If using a gas grill, turn all burners to high and close the lid. When the temperature inside the grill reaches 350° to 400°F, lift the lid, turn off one of the burners, and lower the other burner(s) to medium-high. Place a drip pan under the turned-off burner—this is the indirect-heat area.

5   Set the oiled grill rack in place. Lay the pork on the grill over the drip pan and cover the barbecue (open vents for charcoal). Every 30 minutes of cooking, add 5 more briquets to the mound of coals. Grill until a meat thermometer inserted into the thickest part registers 150°F, about 1 hour. Let the pork rest, covered loosely with foil, about 5 minutes. Remove the strings, slice the pork, and serve immediately.

Makes 10 to 12 servings

1/2 cup pine nuts

1/4 cup chopped fresh rosemary

3 tablespoons Dijon mustard

3 cloves garlic, chopped

1/2 cup extra-virgin olive oil

4 pork tenderloins (each 1/2 to 3/4 pound)

1 teaspoon salt

1/2 teaspoon freshly ground black pepper

Fennel-Brined Pork Chops

Prep and cook time: About 1 hour, plus 4 hours to marinate

1. Combine 1 cup water with the fennel fronds and seeds in a small saucepan and bring to a boil. Remove the fennel mixture from heat and pour into a large bowl. Let cool to room temperature.

2. To the fennel mixture, add 2 1/2 cups water and the salt, sugar, and liqueur, stirring until the salt and sugar dissolve. Pour the mixture into a large resealable plastic bag. Add the pork and seal. Refrigerate for 4 hours, turning the bag occasionally.

3. Prepare a grill for cooking over high heat. First, oil the grill rack. If using a charcoal grill, prepare a solid bed of hot coals. If using a gas grill, preheat to high (you can hold your hand 1 to 2 inches above grill level only 2 to 3 seconds).

4. Remove the pork from the bag and discard the brine. Pat the pork dry with paper towels and coat lightly with olive oil. Combine the rosemary, pepper, and garlic and rub it evenly over both sides of the pork. Lay the pork chops on the grill rack. If using a gas grill, close the lid. Grill, turning once, until just barely pink in the center (cut to test), about 3 minutes on each side. Let the chops stand 5 minutes before serving.

Makes 4 servings

- 1/2 cup chopped fennel fronds
- 1 tablespoon fennel seeds
- 1/4 cup kosher salt
- 1/4 cup sugar
- 2 tablespoons sambuca or other anise-flavored liqueur
- 4 (4-ounce) boneless center-cut loin pork chops (about 3/4 inch thick)
- Olive oil
- 2 teaspoons chopped fresh rosemary
- 1 teaspoon freshly ground black pepper
- 2 cloves garlic, minced

....

Notes from The Sunset Grill

These chops are made with both fennel seeds and fresh fennel fronds, the flowery ends of the fennel bulb. (Once you remove the fronds, you can grill the fennel bulb, see page 80, and serve it alongside the chops if you like.) If you can't find fresh fennel, substitute an additional 2 tablespoons of fennel seeds for the fronds.

Grilled Pork Chops with Fiery Salsa

Prep and cook time: About 30 minutes

1 Make the Fiery Salsa: Combine the tomato, onion, avocado, cilantro, Sriracha, lemon juice, and fish sauce in a bowl. Set aside.

2 Prepare a grill for cooking over medium-high heat. First, oil the grill rack. If using a charcoal grill, prepare a solid bed of medium-hot coals. If using a gas grill, preheat to high and close the lid, then open the lid and lower the heat to medium-high (you can hold your hand 1 to 2 inches above grill level only 3 to 4 seconds).

3 Meanwhile, lightly brush the chops with olive oil, evenly coating both sides. Combine the sugar, garlic powder, coriander, salt, and pepper and sprinkle evenly over both sides of the pork chops. Lay the meat on the grill rack. If using a gas grill, close the lid. Grill, turning once, until just barely pink in the center (cut to test), about 4 minutes on each side. Let the pork chops stand 5 minutes, then serve with salsa on the side.

Makes 4 servings

Olive oil

4 (4-ounce) boneless center-cut loin pork chops (about 1/2 inch thick)

1 teaspoon sugar

3/4 teaspoon garlic powder

1/2 teaspoon ground coriander

1/4 teaspoon salt

1/8 teaspoon freshly ground black pepper

FIERY SALSA

1 1/2 cups diced tomato

1/3 cup diced red onion

1/4 cup diced avocado

1 tablespoon chopped fresh cilantro

1 1/2 tablespoons Sriracha (hot chile sauce, such as *Huy Fong*)

2 teaspoons fresh lemon juice

1/2 teaspoon fish sauce

Grilled Pork Chops Stuffed with Prunes and Prosciutto

Prep and cook time: About 1 hour

1 Soak the prunes in boiling water for 5 minutes. Drain the prunes. Wrap 2 prune halves in each slice of prosciutto.

2 Combine the fennel seeds, paprika, sage, rosemary, kosher salt, crushed red pepper, and black pepper in a small bowl.

3 Cut a horizontal slit through the thickest portion of each pork chop to form a pocket. Stuff 1 prune-prosciutto package into each pocket. Lightly brush the chops with olive oil, evenly coating both sides. Sprinkle the chops with the fennel mixture and set aside.

4 Prepare a grill for cooking over high heat. First, oil the grill rack. If using a charcoal grill, prepare a solid bed of hot coals. If using a gas grill, preheat to high (you can hold your hand 1 to 2 inches above grill level only 2 to 3 seconds).

5 Lay the pork chops on the grill rack. If using a gas grill, close the lid. Grill, turning once, until just barely pink in the center (cut to test), about 4 minutes on each side. Let the chops stand 5 minutes. Combine the vinegar and molasses, brush over the pork chops, and serve immediately.

Makes 4 servings

4 pitted prunes, halved

2 very thin slices prosciutto (about $3/4$ ounce), halved

$1/2$ **teaspoon crushed fennel seeds**

$1/2$ **teaspoon paprika**

$1/2$ **teaspoon chopped fresh sage**

$1/2$ **teaspoon chopped fresh rosemary**

$1/4$ **teaspoon kosher salt**

$1/4$ **teaspoon crushed red pepper**

$1/4$ **teaspoon freshly ground black pepper**

4 (4-ounce) boneless center-cut loin pork chops (about $3/4$ inch thick)

Olive oil

2 teaspoons balsamic vinegar

2 teaspoons molasses

Spiced Pulled-Pork Sandwiches

Prep and cook time: About 2½ hours, plus at least 2 hours to marinate

1 Rinse the pork and pat it dry. In a food processor, purée the green onions, garlic, chiles, tomato paste, brown sugar, allspice, thyme, salt, and pepper until finely chopped. Add the vinegar and blend until smooth. Scrape the mixture into a large resealable plastic bag. Add the pork and chill at least 2 hours or up to 1 day.

2 Put the wood chips in a bowl, cover with water, and soak for 30 minutes. Prepare a grill for cooking over indirect heat. First, oil the grill rack. If using a charcoal grill, light 50 to 60 briquets and let burn until covered with ash, about 25 minutes, then mound them to one side. Place a drip pan on the side cleared of coals. Pour an inch of warm water into the drip pan and scatter the soaked wood chips over the coals. If using a gas grill, turn all burners to high and close the lid. When the temperature inside the grill reaches 400°F, turn off one of the burners and lower the other burner(s) to medium. Place a drip pan under the turned-off burner. Pour an inch of warm water into the drip pan and put the wood chips in grill's smoker box, or wrap the chips loosely in foil, poke several holes in the foil package, and place it directly over the hot burners.

3 Set the oiled grill rack in place. Remove the pork from the marinade. Scrape all the marinade into a small saucepan. Add 1 cup water and bring to a boil over high heat until thickened slightly, about 5 minutes. Remove ¾ cup of the marinade for basting and set the rest aside for serving. Place the pork over the drip pan and cook the pork, trying to maintain a grill temperature of 325°F, basting every 15 minutes or so with the ¾ cup marinade, until the pork reaches an internal temperature of 185°F, about 1¾ hours.

4 Remove the pork to a piece of foil, wrap it tightly, and let stand 30 minutes. With a fork or your fingers, pull the pork into thin shreds, removing and discarding the fat. Stir the shredded pork into the reserved marinade and season with salt and pepper to taste. Spoon the pulled pork into the rolls and serve.

Makes 8 to 10 sandwiches

1½ pounds boned pork shoulder or butt, fat trimmed

4 ounces green onions, rinsed, ends trimmed, and coarsely chopped

2 cloves garlic, peeled

2 fresh Fresno or other hot green chiles (about 1 ounce total), rinsed, stemmed, and seeded

2 tablespoons tomato paste

2 tablespoons brown sugar

2 teaspoons ground allspice

1 teaspoon ground dried thyme

1 teaspoon salt, plus more to taste

½ teaspoon freshly ground black pepper, plus more to taste

¼ cup cider vinegar

2 cups mesquite chips

8 to 10 soft dinner rolls (about 1 ounce each), sliced in half horizontally

Classic Western Burgers

Prep and cook time: About 1 hour

1 Prepare the Special Slaw: In a large bowl, mix together the yogurt, mayonnaise, pickle relish, chili sauce, and mustard. Add the cabbage, carrots, bell pepper, and green onions, and mix well. Season to taste with salt and pepper.

2 In a 10- to 12-inch frying pan over medium-high heat, cook the bacon, in batches if necessary, turning occasionally, until browned on both sides and crisp, 8 to 10 minutes. With tongs, transfer the bacon to paper towels to drain. Reserve the bacon fat in the pan. When cool, break each bacon slice in half.

3 Meanwhile, in a large bowl, beat the eggs, milk, onion, garlic, $1\frac{1}{4}$ teaspoons salt, and $\frac{1}{2}$ teaspoon pepper to blend. Add the beef and the bread crumbs and mix gently. Form into 10 equal patties, each about $4\frac{1}{2}$ inches wide. Brush the onion slices lightly on both sides with reserved bacon fat. Discard remaining fat.

4 Prepare a grill for cooking over medium-high heat. First, oil the grill rack. If using a charcoal grill, prepare a solid bed of medium-hot coals. If using a gas grill, preheat to high and close the lid, then open the lid and lower the heat to medium-high (you can hold your hand 1 to 2 inches above grill level only 3 to 4 seconds). Lay the burgers and onion slices on the grill rack. If using a gas grill, close the lid. Cook the burgers and the onions, turning once, until the burgers are browned on both sides and done to your liking (cut to test), about 7 minutes total for medium-rare.

5 About 2 minutes before the burgers are done, top each with a slice of cheese. Lay the buns, cut side down, on the grill and toast 1 to 2 minutes.

6 Assemble the burgers, topping each with a grilled onion slice, 2 pieces of bacon, and a spoonful of Special Slaw. Add salt and pepper to taste and serve immediately.

Makes 10 servings

10 slices thick-cut bacon

2 large eggs

$\frac{2}{3}$ cup milk

1 onion, peeled and minced

2 teaspoons minced garlic

About $1\frac{1}{4}$ teaspoons salt

About $\frac{1}{2}$ teaspoon freshly ground black pepper

3 pounds ground beef sirloin or chuck

1 cup soft bread crumbs

10 slices red onion (each $\frac{1}{4}$ inch thick and 3 to 4 inches wide)

10 slices extra-sharp white or yellow cheddar cheese (each 4 by 4 inches)

10 hamburger buns, split in half

SPECIAL SLAW

$\frac{1}{2}$ cup plain yogurt

$\frac{1}{4}$ cup mayonnaise

3 tablespoons sweet pickle relish

2 tablespoons tomato-based chili sauce

1 tablespoon coarse-grain Dijon mustard

10 cups finely shredded green cabbage

2 cups finely shredded carrots

$\frac{3}{4}$ cup diced red bell pepper

$\frac{1}{2}$ cup thinly sliced green onions, including tops

Salt and freshly ground black pepper

Chinese Five Spice Burgers

Prep and cook time: About 45 minutes

1. Pour the oil into an 8- to 10-inch nonstick frying pan over high heat. When the oil is hot, add the mushrooms and stir until lightly browned, about 4 minutes. Stir in the green onions and plum sauce and remove from the heat.

2. In a bowl, gently mix the ground beef with the soy sauce, sesame oil, garlic, Chinese five spice powder, and ginger. Shape the beef mixture into 4 equal patties, each about 1/2 inch thick.

3. Prepare a grill for cooking over medium-high heat. First, oil the grill rack. If using a charcoal grill, prepare a solid bed of medium-hot coals. If using a gas grill, preheat to high and close the lid, then open the lid and lower the heat to medium-high (you can hold your hand 1 to 2 inches above grill level only 3 to 4 seconds). Lay the patties on the grill rack. If using a gas grill, close the lid.

4. Cook the burgers, turning once, until browned on both sides and done to your liking (cut to test), about 7 minutes total for medium-rare. Lay the buns, cut side down, on the grill and toast 1 to 2 minutes.

5. Assemble the burgers, using the lettuce leaves and the sautéed mushroom mixture. Add salt to taste and serve immediately.

Makes 4 servings

About 1 tablespoon olive oil

1 cup thinly sliced mushrooms (3 1/2 ounces)

1/3 cup thinly sliced green onions, including tops

6 tablespoons prepared Chinese plum sauce

1 pound ground beef sirloin or chuck

2 tablespoons soy sauce

1 teaspoon Asian (toasted) sesame oil

1 teaspoon minced garlic

1/2 teaspoon Chinese five spice powder (see Notes)

1/4 teaspoon ground ginger

4 sesame seed–topped hamburger buns, cut in half horizontally

Lettuce leaves, rinsed and crisped

Salt

Notes from The Sunset Grill

You can now find Chinese five spice blends in the spice section of most supermarkets, where you'll also find prepared plum sauce and Asian sesame oil. If you can't find five spice powder, substitute 1/8 teaspoon each ground cinnamon, ground cloves, ground ginger, and anise seeds.

Gold Nugget Burgers

Prep and cook time: About 1 hour

1. Prepare the Sweet-and-Spicy Sauce: In a 1¹/2- to 2-quart pan, combine the ketchup, orange juice, Worcestershire sauce, raisins, ginger, garlic, lime juice, and cayenne. Bring to a boil over medium-high heat, then reduce heat so mixture barely simmers. Cook, uncovered, stirring often, until sauce is thick and reduced to 1 cup, about 20 minutes. Purée the mixture in a blender until smooth and let cool.

2. Prepare the Guacamole: Pit and peel the avocado. In a bowl, coarsely mash the avocado with a potato masher. Stir in the cilantro, lime juice, chile, garlic, and salt to taste.

3. In a bowl, gently mix the ground beef, ¹/2 teaspoon salt, and ¹/4 teaspoon pepper. Shape the beef mixture into 8 equal patties, each about 4 inches wide. Top each of 4 patties with 2 slices of cheese. Lay the remaining patties on top and press the edges of the beef together to seal.

4. Prepare a grill for cooking over medium-high heat. First, oil the grill rack. If using a charcoal grill, prepare a solid bed of medium-hot coals. If using a gas grill, preheat to high and close the lid, then open the lid and lower the heat to medium-high (you can hold your hand 1 to 2 inches above grill level only 3 to 4 seconds). Lay the burgers on the grill rack. If using a gas grill, close the lid.

5. Cook the burgers and the onions, turning once, until the burgers are browned on both sides and done to your liking (cut to test), about 7 minutes total for medium-rare. Lay the buns, cut side down, on the grill and cook until lightly toasted, 1 to 2 minutes.

6. Spread the Sweet-and-Spicy Sauce on the bun bottoms. Add the lettuce, tomatoes, burgers, onions, and Guacamole. Set the bun tops in place and serve immediately.

Makes 4 servings

- 1¹/2 pounds ground beef sirloin or chuck
- ¹/2 teaspoon salt and ¹/4 teaspoon freshly ground black pepper
- 8 slices cheddar cheese
- 1 red onion, peeled and cut into ¹/2-inch-thick slices
- 4 Kaiser, onion, or crusty round rolls (4-inch), split
- 1¹/2 cups shredded iceberg lettuce
- 1 firm-ripe tomato, cored and thinly sliced

SWEET-AND-SPICY SAUCE

- 3/4 cup ketchup
- ¹/2 cup fresh orange juice
- ¹/4 cup Worcestershire sauce
- ¹/4 cup raisins
- 1 tablespoon minced fresh ginger
- 1 tablespoon minced garlic
- 2 tablespoons fresh lime juice
- ¹/2 teaspoon cayenne

GUACAMOLE

- 1 large ripe avocado
- 2 tablespoons chopped fresh cilantro
- 1 tablespoon fresh lime juice
- 2 to 3 teaspoons minced fresh jalapeño chile
- 1 clove garlic, minced
- Salt

Korean Barbecued Short Ribs

Prep and cook time: About 1 hour, plus at least 1 hour to marinate

1 Trim the thick outer layer of fat from the ribs and discard. Rinse the ribs and pat them dry. Butterfly the meat lengthwise on the meaty side of each rib, without cutting it free from the bone.

2 In a glass measuring cup, combine the soy sauce, sherry, sugar, and ginger. Divide evenly between two large resealable plastic bags. Add half of the short ribs to each bag, seal, and turn over to coat the meat with the marinade. Put the ribs in the refrigerator to marinate at least 1 hour or up to 24 hours, turning several times.

3 Prepare a grill for cooking over high heat. First, oil the grill rack. If using a charcoal grill, prepare a solid bed of hot coals. If using a gas grill, preheat to high (you can hold your hand 1 to 2 inches above grill level only 2 to 3 seconds).

4 Remove the ribs and discard the marinade. Lay the ribs, butterflied so the meat is flat, on the grill rack. Cover the grill, opening the vents if using charcoal. Cook the ribs, turning once, until browned and cooked through, about 4 minutes on each side. Pile the ribs on a platter and serve.

Makes 4 servings

4 pounds beef short ribs

1/4 cup soy sauce

1/4 cup dry sherry

1 tablespoon sugar

1 tablespoon minced fresh ginger

Notes from The Sunset Grill
Buy ribs with the bones whole, not cracked. These ribs are delicious served with steamed rice and braised bitter greens or bok choy.

Hot Flank Steak Salad with Chinese Black Bean Dressing

Prep and cook time: About 1¹/₂ hours

1 Trim excess fat from the steak. Rinse the meat, pat dry, and rub with 1 tablespoon soy sauce and the oil.

2 Prepare a grill for cooking over very high heat. First, oil the grill rack. If using a charcoal grill, prepare a solid bed of very hot coals. If using a gas grill, preheat to the highest heat (you can hold your hand 1 to 2 inches above grill level only 1 to 2 seconds).

3 Lay the steak on the grill rack. If using a gas grill, close the lid. Cook the steak, turning once, until firm when pressed on the thin end but still quite pink in the center (cut to check), about 4 minutes on each side. Transfer the steak to a plate and let cool at least 30 minutes.

4 On a board with a sharp knife, cut the steak across the grain, straight up and down, into very thin slices, keeping slices in place. Cut the steak lengthwise to divide the slices into halves or quarters.

5 In a large frying pan, combine the remaining 4 tablespoons soy sauce, the broth, black beans, sherry, ginger, vinegar, cornstarch mixture, and brown sugar. Stir the dressing over high heat until boiling. Add the steak and its juices and stir until hot, about 2 minutes. Remove from the heat.

6 Put the peanuts in a resealable plastic bag and coarsely crush with a meat mallet or the bottom of a small, heavy skillet. Stack the lettuce leaves and cut crosswise into thin slices.

7 Divide the lettuce equally among 6 wide salad or soup bowls and spoon the hot steak and dressing over the greens. Sprinkle with the bell pepper, green onions, and peanuts. Garnish with the cilantro and serve immediately.

Makes 6 servings

1¹/₂ to 1³/₄ pounds flank steak

5 tablespoons soy sauce

1 tablespoon vegetable oil

1 cup reduced-sodium chicken broth

¹/₄ cup rinsed and drained salted fermented black beans

3 tablespoons dry sherry

3 tablespoons minced fresh ginger

6 tablespoons rice vinegar

2 tablespoons cornstarch blended smoothly with 2 tablespoons water

1¹/₂ tablespoons light brown sugar

¹/₂ cup salted peanuts

About 15 large romaine lettuce leaves

³/₄ cup finely diced red bell pepper

¹/₂ cup thinly sliced green onions, including tops

¹/₂ cup cilantro leaves

Flank Steak Tortitas with Chipotle Crema

Prep and cook time: About 1¼ hours

1   Prepare the Chipotle Crema: Wearing kitchen gloves, pull out and discard the seeds and veins from the chiles, reserving the adobo sauce, then mince the chiles. In a small bowl, mix the chiles, adobo sauce, and the crema. Set aside for serving.

2   Rinse the flank steak and pat it dry. In a blender or food processor, mix the garlic, green onions, jalapeño chiles, cumin, oregano, and vinegar until coarsely puréed. Rub over the meat.

3   Peel the red onion and cut into slices ½ inch thick. Rub the slices lightly with the olive oil. Cut the rolls almost in half horizontally, leaving them attached on one side.

4   Prepare a grill for cooking over very high heat. First, oil the grill rack. If using a charcoal grill, prepare a solid bed of very hot coals. If using a gas grill, preheat to the highest heat (you can hold your hand 1 to 2 inches above grill level only 1 to 2 seconds).

5   Lay the steak and onion slices on the grill rack. If using a gas grill, close the lid. Cook the meat, turning once, until done to your liking (cut to test), 6 to 7 minutes on each side for medium-rare, and about 8 minutes on each side for medium. Meanwhile, grill the onion slices, turning once, until lightly browned, about 7 minutes on each side. Transfer the meat and onions to a carving board and let meat stand at least 5 minutes before carving.

6   The beef can be served hot, warm, or at room temperature. To serve, cut the beef across the grain into thin slices. Tuck the slices of meat and pieces of red onion into the rolls. Spoon a dollop of the Chipotle Crema on top and add the tomatillo slices. Pile the sandwiches in a basket or on a platter and serve.

Makes 8 servings

....

Notes from The Sunset Grill
Look for Mexican crema in Latino grocery stores or substitute crème fraîche or sour cream.

1½ to 1¾ pounds beef flank steak

¼ cup chopped garlic

½ cup chopped green onions, including tops

2 tablespoons minced fresh jalapeño chiles

1 teaspoon ground cumin

2 tablespoons fresh oregano leaves or 1 teaspoon dried oregano

2 tablespoons balsamic vinegar

1 red onion

About 2 teaspoons olive oil

16 small round rolls

6 fresh tomatillos, papery skin removed, thinly sliced

CHIPOTLE CREMA

2 canned chipotle chiles in adobo sauce

1½ cups Mexican crema (see Notes)

Gin and Spice Flank Steak

Prep and cook time: About 45 minutes

1 In a spice grinder, grind 2 teaspoons juniper berries, the allspice, and peppercorns until coarsely ground. Add salt and pulse to mix.

2 Trim the fat from the steak. Rinse the meat, pat dry, and rub all over with olive oil. Pat and rub spice mixture on both sides.

3 In a 2-quart pot, bring the broth and the remaining 2 teaspoons juniper berries to a boil over high heat and boil until reduced by 3/4. Add the cream and 2 tablespoons gin and boil over medium-high heat until reduced by half.

4 Prepare a grill for cooking over very high heat. First, oil the grill rack. If using a charcoal grill, prepare a solid bed of very hot coals. If using a gas grill, preheat to the highest heat (you can hold your hand 1 to 2 inches above grill level only 1 to 2 seconds).

5 Lay the steak on the grill rack. If using a gas grill, close the lid. Cook, turning over the steak halfway through, until firm when pressed on thin end but still quite pink inside (cut to check), 8 to 10 minutes. Meanwhile, reheat the gin sauce over medium-low heat and, if more zip is desired, add 1 tablespoon gin.

6 Transfer the steak to a carving board with a well (to catch juices). With a sharp knife, carve the steak across the grain into thin, wide slices, holding the knife at a low angle to the meat. Transfer the meat to a warm platter. Scrape the drippings and juice from the board into the gin sauce. Serve the meat slices with the sauce.

Makes 6 servings

....

Notes from The Sunset Grill
Sealed airtight, the spice blend keeps for several months. You can make the steak through step 2 up to 6 hours ahead and chill, covered. While you're at it, make the sauce up to 6 hours ahead and also cover and chill.

4 teaspoons dried juniper berries

1 1/2 teaspoons whole allspice

1 1/2 teaspoons black peppercorns

1 teaspoon kosher salt

1 flank steak (1 1/2 to 1 3/4 pounds)

1 tablespoon olive oil

1 cup reduced-sodium beef or chicken broth

3/4 cup heavy cream

2 to 3 tablespoons gin

Korean Noodles with Grilled Beef

Prep and cook time: About 1 1/4 hours, plus at least 30 minutes to marinate

1 Rinse the beef and pat dry. Cut the steak across the grain, into 1/4-inch-thick slices and place them in a large bowl. Add the soy sauce, green onions, sesame oil, sugar, and garlic and mix. Cover and chill at least 30 minutes or up to 4 hours.

2 Meanwhile, in a large covered pan over high heat, bring 2 quarts water to a boil. Put the noodles in the water and stir to separate. Cover, remove from the heat, and let stand until soft, 3 to 5 minutes. Drain and cut the noodles into 6-inch lengths. Place the mushrooms in a small bowl with hot water to cover. Let stand until soft, 15 minutes. Lift the mushrooms from the soaking liquid and squeeze dry. Cut off the stems and discard. Cut the caps into 1/4-inch strips. Trim the ends from the whole green onions and cut into 2-inch lengths, including the green tops. In a large nonstick frying pan over medium-high heat, stir 2 teaspoons sesame oil and the yellow onion until slightly softened, 2 minutes. Pour the onions into a large serving bowl. Add 2 teaspoons more sesame oil, the carrots, and green onion to the pan. Stir until the green onions are slightly wilted, about 2 minutes. Add to the bowl with the yellow onion. Add 2 teaspoons more sesame oil, the mushrooms, and the green beans to the pan. Stir until the mushrooms are lightly browned, about 4 minutes. Add to the bowl with the other vegetables, season with salt and pepper, and set aside.

3 If using a charcoal grill, prepare a solid bed of hot coals. If using a gas grill, preheat to high. Spread the beef slices, on an oiled grill rack. If using a gas grill, close the lid. Cook the beef, turning once, until browned, 2 to 3 minutes on each side. Chop the beef into pieces, and add to the bowl of vegetables. In the large nonstick frying pan, over medium-high heat, add 2 table-spoons sesame oil, the drained noodles, 3 tablespoons soy sauce, 2 teaspoons sugar, and 1/4 teaspoon freshly ground black pepper. Toss and stir until the noodles are hot, about 3 minutes. Pour the noodles into the bowl with the vegetables and beef, sprinkle with the sliced green onions and toasted sesame seeds, and serve.

Makes 6 servings

6 ounces dried bean threads (*saifun*)

1 ounce dried shiitake mushrooms

4 tablespoons Asian (toasted) sesame oil

5 tablespoons soy sauce

3 whole plus 2 tablespoons sliced green onions

1 tablespoon sugar

1 clove garlic, minced

1 yellow onion, peeled and cut into 1/4-inch slices

1 cup coarsely shredded carrots

1 cup green beans, cut on the diagonal into 1/4-inch slices

Salt and freshly ground black pepper

1 tablespoon toasted sesame seeds

GRILLED BEEF

1/2 pound beef flank steak

1/4 cup soy sauce

3 tablespoons thinly sliced green onions

1 tablespoon Asian (toasted) sesame oil

About 1 1/2 tablespoons sugar

1 to 2 cloves garlic, minced

Beef Satay

Prep and cook time: About 1 hour

1   If you are using wood skewers, soak 12 in water for 30 minutes. Prepare the Spice Paste.

2   Cut the meat into ³/4-inch chunks. Mix the Spice Paste with the sugar, then stir in the chunks of meat. Thread the meat onto the skewers.

3   Prepare a grill for cooking over high heat. First, oil the grill rack. If using a charcoal grill, prepare a solid bed of hot coals. If using a gas grill, preheat to high (you can hold your hand 1 to 2 inches above grill level only 2 to 3 seconds). Lay the skewers on the grill rack. If using a gas grill, close the lid. Cook, turning once, until nicely browned, 2 to 3 minutes on each side. Serve hot or at room temperature.

Makes 4 to 6 main-course or 8 to 10 first-course servings

¹/4 **cup Spice Paste, see page 95**

1¹/2 **pounds boned beef top sirloin, fat-trimmed**

2 **tablespoons chopped palm sugar or brown sugar**

Notes from The Sunset Grill

As an alternative to the Spice Paste, you can use ¹/4 cup purchased Thai red curry paste mixed with 2 tablespoons olive oil. Stir the sauce in a 6- to 8-inch frying pan over medium heat until fragrant, about 5 minutes, then add the sugar.

Warm Steak Salad with Artichokes and Arugula

Prep and cook time: About 1 1/2 hours

1 In a large bowl, combine 1 quart water and the lemon juice. Rinse the artichokes, then snap off and discard the leaves nearest the base. Stop when you get down to the leaves that are half green and half yellow. Trim the green tops from the artichokes. Cut the stems flush with the bases. Cut the artichokes in half lengthwise and if the center is fuzzy or prickly, scrape it out. Drop the artichokes in the lemon water as you trim them. Lift out the artichokes and cut into very thin slices with a sharp knife. Return the slices to the lemon water.

2 Rinse the steak, pat dry, and trim off any excess surface fat. Rub 1 tablespoon olive oil all over the steak. Season the steak generously with salt and pepper.

3 Prepare a grill for cooking over medium-high heat. First, oil the grill rack. If using a charcoal grill, prepare a solid bed of medium-hot coals. If using a gas grill, preheat to high and close the lid, then open the lid and lower the heat to medium-high (you can hold your hand 1 to 2 inches above grill level only 3 to 4 seconds). Lay the steak on the grill rack. If using a gas grill, close the lid. Cook the steak, turning once, until rare (cut to test), about 6 minutes on each side, or until medium-rare, about 8 minutes on each side. Put the steak on a cutting board, cover loosely with foil, and let rest for about 5 minutes.

4 Meanwhile, in a large bowl, mix 1 tablespoon *each* olive oil and balsamic vinegar. Mix in the arugula, then pile it on a large platter. To the bowl, add 1 more tablespoon *each* olive oil and balsamic vinegar. Drain the artichoke slices and add them to the bowl. Mix gently and season to taste with salt and pepper. Spread the artichokes and the dressing evenly over the arugula. Cut the steak crosswise into 1/4-inch-thick slices and lay, overlapping slightly, on top of the artichokes. With a vegetable peeler, shave curls of cheese on top of the steak, drizzle with 2 tablespoons olive oil, and serve.

Makes 6 to 8 servings

2 tablespoons fresh lemon juice

12 ounces baby artichokes

2 boned beef top loin steaks or 1 sirloin steak (2 inches thick, 2 1/2 to 3 pounds total)

About 5 tablespoons extra-virgin olive oil

Salt and freshly ground black pepper

2 tablespoons balsamic vinegar

8 ounces baby or bite-size pieces arugula leaves or tender watercress sprigs, rinsed and crisped

About 2 ounces parmesan cheese

Peppered Steak with Horseradish-Chive Cream

Prep and cook time: About 45 minutes

1 Prepare a grill for cooking over medium-high heat. First, oil the grill rack. If using a charcoal grill, prepare a solid bed of medium-hot coals. If using a gas grill, preheat to high and close the lid, then open the lid and lower the heat to medium-high (you can hold your hand 1 to 2 inches above grill level only 3 to 4 seconds).

2 Meanwhile, in a small bowl, combine the sour cream, chives, horseradish, and Worcestershire sauce, stirring until well blended, then cover and chill until ready to serve.

3 Place the steak between 2 sheets of heavy-duty plastic wrap, and pound to 1/4-inch thickness using a meat mallet or small heavy skillet. In another small bowl, combine the pepper, vinegar, salt, and garlic. Rub the steak with the vinegar mixture.

4 Lay the steak on the grill rack. If using a gas grill, close the lid. Cook the steak, turning once, until rare (cut to test), about 4 minutes on each side, or until medium-rare, about 6 minutes on each side. Put the steak on a cutting board, cover loosely with foil, and let rest for about 5 minutes. Cut the steak crosswise into 1/4-inch-thick slices and serve immediately with the horseradish cream on the side.

Makes 4 servings

1/2 **cup sour cream**

2 **tablespoons chopped fresh chives**

1 **tablespoon prepared horseradish**

1 **teaspoon Worcestershire sauce**

1 **pound beef sirloin steak**

1 **tablespoon freshly ground black pepper**

2 **tablespoons balsamic vinegar**

1/2 **teaspoon salt**

2 **cloves garlic, minced**

Tenderloin Steaks with Gorgonzola Butter

Prep and cook time: About 1 hour

1 Rinse the steaks and pat them dry. Place the steaks in a 1-gallon resealable plastic bag. Set the onion slices in a single layer on a plate. Drizzle 2 tablespoons port and 1 teaspoon oil over the onions, cover, and set aside. Pour the remaining port and oil over the meat and seal the bag. Turn to coat the steaks. Let stand at least 30 minutes, or chill the meat up to 2 hours.

2 Meanwhile, prepare a grill for cooking over medium-high heat. First, oil the grill rack. If using a charcoal grill, prepare a solid bed of medium-hot coals. If using a gas grill, preheat to high and close the lid, then open the lid and lower the heat to medium-high (you can hold your hand 1 to 2 inches above grill level only 3 to 4 seconds).

3 In a small bowl, with a wooden spoon, beat the gorgonzola cheese and butter until well blended and creamy. Spoon into a decorative bowl and set aside for serving.

4 Lift the steaks from the marinade and season generously with salt and pepper. Lay the steaks on the grill rack. Discard the marinade. Lay the onion slices around the steaks. If using a gas grill, close the lid. Cook the steaks, turning once, until rare (cut to test), about 6 minutes on each side, or until medium-rare, about 8 minutes on each side. Let the onions cook, turning them once, until lightly browned, about 8 minutes on each side.

5 Transfer the steaks to a platter and top with the grilled onions. Cover loosely with foil and let rest for 5 minutes. Sprinkle the parsley over the steaks and serve, passing the gorgonzola butter on the side.

Makes 4 servings

4 beef tenderloin steaks (about 2 inches thick, 6 to 8 ounces each)

1 red onion, peeled and cut into thick slices

3/4 cup tawny port

2 tablespoons walnut or olive oil

1/4 cup crumbled gorgonzola cheese (1 1/2 ounces), at room temperature

1/4 cup butter, at room temperature

Salt and freshly ground black pepper

2 tablespoons chopped flat-leaf parsley

Orange-Soy Skirt Steaks

Prep and cook time: About 45 minutes, plus 4 hours to chill

1 Rinse the steaks and pat dry. In a 1-gallon resealable plastic bag, combine the steaks, orange juice, soy sauce, garlic, coarse pepper, oregano, and cumin. Seal the bag and chill at least 4 hours or up to 1 day, turning occasionally.

2 Prepare a grill for cooking over high heat. First, oil the grill rack. If using a charcoal grill, prepare a solid bed of hot coals. If using a gas grill, preheat to high (you can hold your hand 1 to 2 inches above grill level only 2 to 3 seconds).

3 Lift the steaks from the marinade. Thread two 18- to 24-inch-long metal skewers parallel through the center of each steak and season generously with salt and pepper. Discard the marinade.

4 Lay the steaks on the grill rack. If using a gas grill, close the lid. Cook the steak, turning once, until rare (cut to test), about 6 minutes on each side, or until medium-rare, about 8 minutes on each side. Transfer the steaks to a platter, remove the skewers, and serve immediately.

Makes 8 to 10 servings

2 beef skirt steaks (2¹/₂ pounds total)

2 cups fresh orange juice

¹/₄ cup soy sauce

4 to 5 cloves garlic, minced

**1 teaspoon coarsely ground black
    pepper**

1 teaspoon dried oregano

¹/₂ teaspoon ground cumin

Salt and freshly ground black pepper

Grilled Green Onions
Slender green onions, softened and lightly charred on the grill, make an attractive and tasty garnish for grilled meats. Trim the green onions, removing roots but leaving ends intact, and brush them with oil. Place over medium heat and grill, turning often, just until grill-marked.

New York Strip Steaks with Orange and Oregano

Prep and cook time: About 1 hour

1 Trim any excess surface fat from the steaks. Rinse the steaks, pat dry, and place them in a 1-gallon resealable plastic bag. Add the orange juice, vinegar, Worcestershire sauce, olive oil, garlic, and 1 1/2 teaspoons coarse pepper. Seal the bag and turn as needed to coat the steaks with the marinade. Chill for at least 30 minutes or up to 1 day.

2 Meanwhile, prepare a grill for cooking over medium-high heat. First, oil the grill rack. If using a charcoal grill, prepare a solid bed of medium-hot coals. If using a gas grill, preheat to high and close the lid, then open the lid and lower the heat to medium-high (you can hold your hand 1 to 2 inches above grill level only 3 to 4 seconds).

3 Lift the steaks from the marinade and lay them on the grill rack. Discard the marinade. If using a gas grill, close the lid. Cook the steak, turning once, until rare (cut to test), about 4 minutes on each side, or until medium-rare, about 6 minutes on each side.

4 Transfer the steaks to plates and let rest in a warm place for 5 minutes. Sprinkle the steaks with the oregano leaves and salt, and serve with the orange wedges to squeeze over the top.

Makes 4 to 6 servings

4 New York strip steaks (about 12 ounces each)

3/4 cup fresh orange juice

1/4 cup red or white wine vinegar

2 tablespoons Worcestershire sauce

1 tablespoon olive oil

2 cloves garlic, minced

About 1 1/2 teaspoons coarsely ground black pepper

1/4 cup fresh oregano or marjoram leaves

Salt

1 orange, cut into four wedges

Tri-Tip with Shiraz and Soy

Prep and cook time: About 40 minutes, plus at least 2 hours to marinate

1 In a 1-gallon resealable plastic bag, combine the Shiraz, soy sauce, oil, vinegar, lemon juice, Worcestershire sauce, mustard, and garlic. Rinse the tri-tip and pat it dry. Add the meat to the bag and seal. Chill at least 2 hours or up to 1 day, turning occasionally.

2 Prepare a grill for cooking over medium heat. First, oil the grill rack. If using a charcoal grill, prepare a solid bed of medium coals. If using a gas grill, preheat to high and close the lid, then open the lid and lower the heat to medium (you can hold your hand 1 to 2 inches above grill level only 4 to 5 seconds).

3 Lift the tri-tip from the marinade and lay on the grill rack. Discard the marinade. If using a gas grill, close the lid. Cook the tri-tip, turning every 5 minutes, until rare (cut to test), about 20 minutes, or until medium-rare, about 30 minutes.

4 Remove the meat from the grill, cover loosely with foil, and let rest 5 minutes. Cut the meat across the grain into thin slices and serve.

Makes 8 to 10 servings

3/4 cup Shiraz (Syrah) wine

2/3 cup soy sauce

1/4 cup olive oil

1/4 cup balsamic vinegar

1/4 cup fresh lemon juice

2 tablespoons Worcestershire sauce

2 teaspoons Dijon mustard

1 1/2 teaspoons minced garlic

1 beef tri-tip (about 2 1/2 pounds), fat trimmed

Shiraz

The wine grape known as Shiraz in Australia is the same as the Rhône varietal Syrah, but the difference in names indicates a difference in winemaking style: Shiraz is generally fruitier and juicier than Syrah. A bold, big Shiraz complements this marinade's other strong flavors.

Rib-Eye Steaks with Tomato-Basil Relish

Prep and cook time: About 1 hour

1   Trim any surface fat from the steaks. Rinse the steaks and pat dry, then set them in a single layer on a large plate. In a small bowl, mix 1¹/₂ tablespoons of the vinegar with 1¹/₂ tablespoons of the olive oil. Rub the mixture all over the steaks. Let the steaks stand for at least 15 minutes, or cover and chill up to 4 hours.

2   Meanwhile, core and coarsely chop the tomatoes. In a bowl, mix the tomatoes, basil, garlic, and the remaining balsamic vinegar and olive oil. Season the relish to taste with salt and pepper and set aside until ready to serve.

3   Prepare a grill for cooking over high heat. First, oil the grill rack. If using a charcoal grill, prepare a solid bed of hot coals. If using a gas grill, preheat to high (you can hold your hand 1 to 2 inches above grill level only 2 to 3 seconds).

4   Season the steaks generously with salt and pepper. Lay the steaks on the grill rack. If using a gas grill, close the lid. Cook the steaks, turning once, until medium-rare (cut to test), about 6 minutes on each side. Transfer the steaks to a platter, cover loosely with foil, and let rest 5 minutes. Serve with the tomato-basil relish.

Makes 4 to 8 servings

4 boned beef rib-eye steaks (12 to 16 ounces each)

3 tablespoons balsamic vinegar

3 tablespoons olive oil

1 pound firm-ripe tomatoes

2 tablespoons chopped fresh basil leaves

1 or 2 cloves garlic, minced

Salt and freshly ground black pepper

Grilled T-Bone Steak

Prep and cook time: About 30 minutes

1 Trim any excess surface fat from the steaks. Rinse the steaks and pat them dry.

2 In a small bowl, mix the wine, mustard, shallots, olive oil, tarragon, and salt and pepper to taste. Spread the mixture all over the steaks and stack them on a large plate. Let the steaks stand at room temperature for 30 minutes, or cover and chill up to 1 day.

3 Meanwhile, prepare a grill for cooking over high heat. First, oil the grill rack. If using a charcoal grill, prepare a solid bed of hot coals. If using a gas grill, preheat to high (you can hold your hand 1 to 2 inches above grill level only 2 to 3 seconds).

4 Lay the steaks on the grill rack. If using a gas grill, close the lid. Cook the steaks, turning once, until medium-rare (cut to test), about 6 minutes on each side.

5 Transfer the steaks to a platter, cover loosely with foil, and let rest 5 minutes. Garnish the steaks with watercress and serve.

Makes 4 servings

4 beef T-bone steaks (1 to 1¹/₄ pounds each)

¹/₃ cup dry red wine

3 tablespoons Dijon mustard

2 tablespoons minced shallots

2 tablespoons olive oil

1¹/₂ tablespoons chopped fresh tarragon

Salt and freshly ground black pepper

2 cups tender sprigs watercress (about 2 ounces), rinsed and crisped

Fresh Tarragon
This summer herb, with its tender spear-shaped leaves and aromatic aniselike flavor, is often used in classic French cooking. Dried tarragon lacks the fresh leaves' delicacy, so if you can't find fresh tarragon for this recipe, substitute another favorite fresh herb, such as parsley or basil.

Mixed Grill with Glazed Nectarines

Prep and cook time: About 1 hour

1. Rinse the chops and pat dry. Trim off and discard any excess surface fat. In a bowl, mix the chops with olive oil, rosemary, garlic, salt, and pepper. Cover and chill at least 15 minutes or up to 2 hours.

2. Meanwhile, prepare the Glazed Nectarines: In a large bowl, stir the vinegar and brown sugar until smooth. Stir in the nectarines and let stand 15 to 30 minutes.

3. Prepare a grill for cooking over high heat. First, oil the grill rack. If using a charcoal grill, prepare a solid bed of hot coals. If using a gas grill, preheat to high (you can hold your hand 1 to 2 inches above grill level only 2 to 3 seconds).

4. Lay the chops and sausages on the grill rack. If using a gas grill, close the lid. Cook the chops, turning once, until browned and still pink in center of thickest part (cut to test), 3 to 4 minutes on each side. Cook the sausages, turning as needed, until browned and no longer pink in the center (cut to test), 10 to 12 minutes total. Lift the nectarines from the marinade, reserving what is left, season to taste with salt and pepper, and lay them on the grill. Cook the nectarines, turning once, until browned, about 2 minutes on each side.

5. Arrange the lamb chops, sausages, and nectarines on a platter. Spoon the reserved nectarine marinade over the top and serve immediately.

Makes 8 servings

8 lamb rib chops (about 3/4 inch thick, 3 to 4 ounces each)

2 tablespoons olive oil

1/3 cup chopped fresh rosemary leaves

3 tablespoons chopped garlic

1/2 teaspoon salt

1/4 teaspoon freshly ground black pepper

8 mild or hot Italian pork sausages (about 2 pounds)

GLAZED NECTARINES

1 tablespoon sherry vinegar or balsamic vinegar

1 tablespoon firmly packed brown sugar

4 large firm-ripe nectarines, pitted and quartered

Salt and freshly ground black pepper

Beef Rib Roast with Yorkshire Pudding

Prep and cook time: About 2¹/₂ hours

1   In a small bowl, mix the garlic, oil, rosemary, savory, thyme, and pepper. Rinse the beef, pat dry, and coat with mixture.

2   Prepare a charcoal grill for cooking over indirect heat (see Notes). First, oil the grill rack. Light 60 briquets and let burn until covered with ash, about 20 to 30 minutes, then push equal amounts to opposite sides of the firegrate. Add 5 more briquets to each mound of coals now and every 30 minutes while cooking. Place a drip pan on the firegrate between the coals. When the barbecue is medium-hot (you can hold your hand at grill level only 3 to 4 seconds), set an 8-inch square foil pan in the center of the firegrate. Set the oiled grill in place. Set the roast, bones side down, on the grill over the drip pan. Cover the barbecue, opening the vents. Cook, turning occasionally, for 45 minutes.

3   Meanwhile, in a blender, mix the milk, flour, eggs, and salt to make a smooth batter.

4   Transfer the roast to a platter. Protecting your hands, lift the grill off and remove the drip pan. Pour the drippings from the drip pan through a fine strainer into a bowl. Return 1 tablespoon of the drippings to the drip pan, discarding the remainder. Return the drip pan to the firegrate and pour in the batter. Replace the grill, set the roast back over the drip pan, cover the barbecue, and continue cooking the roast, turning occasionally, until medium-rare (135°F in the center of the thickest part), 30 to 50 minutes longer. Cook the pudding until well browned, 40 to 50 minutes. Transfer the roast to a platter, cover loosely with foil, and let stand 10 minutes. If the pudding is done before the roast is ready to carve, close the charcoal barbecue vents and leave the pudding in the barbecue to keep warm.

5   Scoop out the pudding from the pan and place it around the roast, garnish with the watercress, and serve.

Makes 6 to 8 servings

About ¹/₄ cup finely chopped garlic cloves

3 tablespoons olive oil

1¹/₂ teaspoons dried rosemary

1¹/₂ teaspoons dried savory

1¹/₂ teaspoons dried thyme

1¹/₂ teaspoons coarsely ground black pepper

1 center-cut beef rib roast (4 to 5 pounds), fat trimmed

1 cup milk

1 cup all-purpose flour

3 eggs

³/₄ teaspoon salt

Melted butter

Watercress sprigs

Notes from The Sunset Grill

We recommend that you use a charcoal grill for this recipe.

Grilled Veal Chops with White Beans and Fennel

Prep and cook time: About 1 hour

1 Trim the stems and root end from the fennel bulb. Pull the green feathery leaves from the stems, reserving 6 large sprigs. Mince the remaining leaves and set them aside. Cut the bulbs in half lengthwise, cut away the core from each half, and cut across into thin slices.

2 Heat 1 tablespoon olive oil and the garlic in a large frying pan over medium-high heat. Add the sliced fennel. Cook, stirring often, until the fennel begins to brown, about 8 minutes. Stir in the tomatoes, 1/2 teaspoon thyme, the red pepper flakes to taste, and the beans. Cook, stirring occasionally, until some of liquid has evaporated and the mixture is slightly thickened, 7 to 10 minutes. Stir in the minced fennel leaves, remove the bean and fennel mixture from the heat, and keep warm.

3 Prepare a grill for cooking over medium-high heat. First, oil the grill rack. If using a charcoal grill, prepare a solid bed of medium-hot coals. If using a gas grill, preheat to high and close the lid, then open the lid and lower the heat to medium-high (you can hold your hand 1 to 2 inches above grill level only 3 to 4 seconds).

4 Meanwhile, in a small bowl, combine the remaining 1 tablespoon oil and 1/2 teaspoon thyme with salt and pepper to taste. Brush the oil all over the chops. Lay the chops on the grill rack. If using a gas grill, close the lid. Cook, turning once, until the chops are medium-rare (cut to test), about 5 minutes on each side.

5 Divide the bean and fennel mixture among 6 dinner plates. Place the chops on the beans, garnish with the parmesan cheese and reserved fennel sprigs, and serve immediately.

Makes 6 servings

1 large fennel bulb, with green feathery leaves attached

2 tablespoons olive oil

1 large clove garlic, minced

1 cup chopped fresh tomatoes or canned tomatoes and their liquid

1 teaspoon dried thyme

1/8 to 1/4 teaspoon red pepper flakes

2 cans (15 ounces each) white beans, drained

Salt and freshly ground black pepper

6 veal rib chops (each 3/4 inch thick), trimmed of fat

2 ounces parmesan cheese, shaved into curls with a vegetable peeler

Mediterranean Lamb Burgers

Prep and cook time: About 1 hour

1 Immerse the onions in ice water for about 30 minutes and drain thoroughly.

2 Meanwhile, in a bowl, mix the lamb with 3 tablespoons mint, 1 tablespoon garlic, 1/2 teaspoon salt, and 1/2 teaspoon pepper. Divide the mixture into 6 equal portions. Shape each portion into a patty and set in a single layer on plastic wrap.

3 Pit and peel the avocado. In another bowl, mash the avocado with the yogurt, the remaining 1 tablespoon mint and 1 teaspoon garlic, and salt and pepper to taste.

4 Prepare a grill for cooking over high heat. First, oil the grill rack. If using a charcoal grill, prepare a solid bed of hot coals. If using a gas grill, preheat to high (you can hold your hand 1 to 2 inches above grill level only 2 to 3 seconds). Lay the lamb patties on the grill rack. If using a gas grill, close the lid. Brown patties on each side, turning once, until no longer pink in center of thickest part (cut to test), 4 to 5 minutes total, or until done to your taste. Grill the rolls as the burgers cook.

5 With a wide spatula, transfer each burger to a roll and dress with the onions, lettuce, and avocado sauce. Serve immediately.

Makes 6 servings

2 cups thinly sliced red onions

1¹/₄ pounds ground lean lamb

¹/₄ cup minced fresh mint leaves

4 teaspoons minced garlic

About ¹/₂ teaspoon salt

About ¹/₂ teaspoon freshly ground black pepper

1 ripe avocado

²/₃ cup plain yogurt

6 ciabatta rolls, cut in half crosswise

Romaine lettuce leaves, rinsed and crisped

Lamb Sandwiches with Grill-Roasted Vegetables

Prep and cook time: About 1½ hours, plus at least 3 hours to marinate

1 In a large bowl, whisk together 2 tablespoons olive oil, the soy sauce, Worcestershire sauce, red wine, 1 teaspoon salt, and ½ teaspoon pepper. Stir in the lamb and refrigerate 3 hours or overnight.

2 Prepare a grill for cooking over indirect heat. First, oil the grill rack. If using a charcoal grill, light 50 to 60 briquets and let burn until covered with ash, 20 to 30 minutes, then mound to one side. If using a gas grill, turn all burners to high and close lid. When temperature inside grill reaches 350° to 400°F, lift the lid and turn off one of the burners.

3 In a large bowl, toss the bell peppers, onions, eggplant, zucchini, and tomatoes with the remaining 7 tablespoons olive oil, 2 teaspoons salt, 1 teaspoon pepper, and the garlic. Transfer the vegetables to a rimmed baking sheet. Put the baking sheet on the indirect-heat area and cook the vegetables, tossing them every 15 minutes or so, until almost tender, about 45 minutes. Drizzle the vegetables with the balsamic vinegar, toss to coat, and cook 15 minutes more. Remove the vegetables from the grill and let cool.

4 Toast the walnuts in a medium frying pan over low heat on the stovetop, tossing frequently, until golden brown and fragrant, about 10 minutes. Add the walnuts to the cooled vegetables and then toss in the feta.

5 Prepare the grill for the lamb: If using charcoal, add about 5 briquets (if the coals look significantly burned down) to bring the heat back to medium-high. If using gas, turn all burners to medium-high. Skewer the lamb onto 4 metal skewers (10 to 12 inches long) and grill directly over the heat about 5 minutes per side for medium. With a fork, push the lamb off the skewers and into a bowl. Warm the pita breads on the grill while the lamb is cooking. Spoon the vegetable mixture into a halved pita, top with the lamb, and serve.

Makes 4 or 5 regular-size or 8 to 10 mini pita sandwiches

½ cup plus 1 tablespoon extra-virgin olive oil

¼ cup soy sauce

2 tablespoons Worcestershire sauce

½ cup red wine

3 teaspoons kosher salt

1½ teaspoons freshly ground black pepper

2 pounds lamb, cut into 1½-inch chunks

2 red bell peppers, stemmed, seeded, and sliced into ¾-inch-wide wedges

2 peeled red onions, sliced into 1-inch-wide wedges

1 large eggplant, quartered lengthwise and cut into 1-inch-thick slices

2 small zucchini, sliced crosswise into ¼-inch-thick slices

3 Roma tomatoes, quartered lengthwise and seeded

3 cloves garlic, chopped

3 tablespoons balsamic vinegar

¼ cup coarsely chopped walnuts

½ cup crumbled feta cheese

4 or 5 regular-size or 8 to 10 mini pita breads, halved

Grilled Lamb Chops
with Romesco Sauce

Prep and cook time: About 40 minutes

1   Prepare the Romesco Sauce: In a 10- to 12-inch frying pan over medium-high heat, stir the almonds until golden, about 5 minutes. Let the nuts cool, then pulse them in a food processor or blender until finely ground. Set aside.

2   To the frying pan, add the oil, onion, and garlic and stir over medium-high heat until the onion softens, about 5 minutes. Add the tomato, red peppers, pepper flakes, and vinegar. Cook, stirring, until most of the liquid is evaporated, about 4 minutes. Remove from heat and stir in the ground almonds. Add salt and pepper to taste. Pour the Romesco Sauce into a bowl and set aside.

3   Prepare a grill for cooking over high heat. First, oil the grill rack. If using a charcoal grill, prepare a solid bed of hot coals. If using a gas grill, preheat to high (you can hold your hand 1 to 2 inches above grill level only 2 to 3 seconds).

4   Rinse the lamb and pat dry. Trim and discard any excess fat, and season both sides with salt and pepper. Lay the lamb on the grill rack. If using a gas grill, close the lid. Cook, turning once, until the lamb is browned on both sides but still pink in the center of the thickest part (cut to test), 8 to 10 minutes total. Serve immediately with the hot or cool Romesco Sauce.

Makes 4 to 6 servings

12 lamb rib chops (about 3/4 inch thick, 3 to 4 ounces each)

Salt and freshly ground black pepper to taste

ROMESCO SAUCE

2 tablespoons slivered almonds

2 tablespoons olive oil

1 onion, peeled and chopped

2 cloves garlic, minced

1 ripe tomato, cored and chopped

3/4 cup chopped canned red peppers

1/4 to 1/2 teaspoon red pepper flakes

3 tablespoons red wine vinegar

Salt and freshly ground black pepper to taste

Lamb Chops with Mint Chutney and Moroccan Barbecue Sauce

Prep and cook time: About 1 hour, plus at least 4 hours to marinate

1 Prepare the Mint Chutney: In a blender or food processor, purée all of the ingredients until smooth. Set aside.

2 Rinse the lamb chops and pat dry. Place them in a bowl with about 1/4 cup of the chutney and turn to coat. Cover and chill at least 4 hours or up to 1 day. Cover and chill the remaining chutney.

3 Prepare the Moroccan Barbecue Sauce: In a 2- to 3-quart pan, combine all of the sauce ingredients. Bring to a simmer over medium-high heat and cook, stirring occasionally, until the sauce is reduced to about 1 1/4 cups, about 15 minutes. Pour the sauce through a fine strainer into a bowl and keep warm.

4 Prepare a grill for cooking over medium-high heat. First, oil the grill rack. If using a charcoal grill, prepare a solid bed of medium-hot coals. If using a gas grill, preheat to high and close the lid, then open the lid and lower the heat to medium-high (you can hold your hand 1 to 2 inches above grill level only 3 to 4 seconds).

5 Lift the lamb chops from the bowl (discard any chutney in bowl) and sprinkle all over with salt and pepper. Lay the lamb on the grill rack. If using a gas grill, close the lid. Cook chops, turning once, until browned on both sides but still pink in the center (cut to test), 9 to 12 minutes total.

6 Place the chops on plates and drizzle with Moroccan Barbecue Sauce, offering the remaining chutney and sauce alongside.

Makes 4 servings

8 lamb loin chops (about 1 inch thick, 4 ounces each), fat trimmed

Salt and freshly ground black pepper

MINT CHUTNEY

1 cup lightly packed fresh mint leaves

1/2 cup olive oil

1/2 cup chopped green onions

3 tablespoons flat-leaf parsley leaves

1 tablespoon fresh lemon juice

1 clove garlic, peeled

1 teaspoon salt

1/2 teaspoon curry powder

1/4 teaspoon cayenne

MOROCCAN BARBECUE SAUCE

3/4 cup honey

1/2 cup fresh cilantro sprigs

1/3 cup fresh lemon juice

1/4 cup *each* rice vinegar, ketchup, and soy sauce

1 clove garlic and 1 whole star anise

1 cinnamon stick (3 inches long)

3/4 teaspoon black peppercorns

1/4 teaspoon *each* ground ginger, ground cardamom, whole cloves, red pepper flakes, and salt

Lamb Chops Stuffed with Stilton

Prep and cook time: About 1 hour

4 double-bone lamb rib chops (about 2 inches thick, 6 ounces each), fat trimmed from the chop and bones

1/4 cup packed Stilton cheese or other firm blue cheese

Salt and freshly ground black pepper to taste

1 Rinse the chops and pat dry. Make a pocket for the stuffing (see Notes): Insert a sharp knife, with a blade about 1/2 inch wide, horizontally into the center of each chop from the fat side to the bone without piercing the other side. Without enlarging the entry slit or cutting through the chop completely, slide the knife in an arc through the meat to within 1/2 to 1/4 inch of the edge. Remove the knife, reverse the direction of the blade, and reinsert it through the entry hole. Slide the knife in the opposite direction to make the pocket wider. Push your index finger through the entry hole and widen the pocket if it's still too narrow.

2 Firmly push 1 tablespoon cheese into the pocket of each chop. Scrape off any cheese that sticks to the exterior of the chop.

3 Prepare a grill for cooking over indirect heat. First, oil the grill rack. If using a charcoal grill, light 70 briquets and let burn until covered with ash, 20 to 30 minutes, then mound them to one side. Place a drip pan on the side cleared of coals—this is the indirect-heat area. If using a gas grill, turn all burners to high and close the lid. When the temperature is very hot (you can hold your hand at grill level only 1 to 2 seconds), lift the lid and turn off one of the burners. Place a drip pan under the turned-off burner—this is the indirect-heat area. Set the oiled grill rack in place. Lay the stuffed chops, bone side up, on grill, not directly over heat (to avoid flare-ups). Cover the grill; open vents for charcoal. Cook the chops on one side until browned, about 2 minutes (move directly over heat if browning too slowly). Turn the chops and brown the remaining side, about 2 minutes. Turn chops, bone side down, and cook 3 to 5 minutes longer for rare, 7 to 10 minutes longer for medium-well. Season to taste with salt and pepper and serve immediately.

Makes 4 servings

Notes from The Sunset Grill

When stuffing thick chops with a sticky mixture, the trick to keeping the filling in is to keep the opening small—just big enough to push the filling through—but the pocket within the chop larger.

Grilled Lamb Loin
with Cabernet-Mint Sauce

Prep and cooking time: About 2 hours, plus at least 4 hours to marinate

1 Rinse the lamb and pat dry. In an 8- by 10-inch baking dish, mix the chopped garlic, olive oil, vinegar, shallots, thyme, parsley, salt, and pepper. Add the lamb and turn to coat. Cover and chill at least 4 hours or up to 1 day, turning occasionally.

2 While the lamb is marinating, prepare the Cabernet-Mint Sauce: Preheat the oven to 350°F. On a 12- by 12-inch sheet of foil, mix the 20 garlic cloves with the olive oil to coat. Seal the foil around the garlic. Bake the cloves, turning the packet over halfway through baking, until they are very soft when pressed, about 45 minutes. Remove the garlic from the oven, open the foil packet, and let the garlic cool. When the garlic is cool enough to handle, squeeze the soft flesh from the cloves into a bowl. Meanwhile, in a 10- to 12-inch frying pan over high heat, boil the wine until reduced to 1 cup, about 10 minutes. Add the broth and boil, stirring occasionally, until the mixture is reduced to about 1 1/2 cups, about 10 minutes more. Whisk in the 1 tablespoon butter, then stir in the mint and the roasted garlic. Season to taste with salt and pepper. Keep warm over low heat.

3 Prepare a grill for cooking over medium-high heat. First, oil the grill rack. If using a charcoal grill, prepare a solid bed of medium-hot coals. If using a gas grill, preheat to high and close the lid, then open the lid and lower the heat to medium-high. Lift the lamb from the marinade, drain well, and discard the marinade. Lay the lamb on the grill rack. If using a gas grill, close the lid. Turn occasionally until the lamb is browned on all sides and a thermometer inserted in the center of the thickest part reaches 135°F for medium-rare, 20 to 25 minutes, or until done to your liking. Transfer the lamb to a board and let rest 5 minutes before carving. Remove the string from the lamb. Slice the loin crosswise into thin slices and serve immediately with the sauce.

Makes 4 servings

1 fat-trimmed lamb loin, boned, rolled, and tied (about 1 pound after boning)

5 cloves garlic, chopped

1/2 cup extra-virgin olive oil

1/2 cup balsamic vinegar

1/2 cup chopped shallots

2 tablespoons fresh thyme leaves

1 tablespoon chopped flat-leaf parsley

1/2 teaspoon salt

1/4 teaspoon freshly ground black pepper

CABERNET-MINT SAUCE

20 cloves garlic, peeled

1/2 tablespoon extra-virgin olive oil

2 cups Cabernet Sauvignon or other dry red wine

3 cups low-sodium beef broth

1 tablespoon butter

1/4 cup chopped fresh mint leaves

Salt and freshly ground black pepper to taste

DESSERTS

DRINKS

desserts & drinks

Strawberries and Oranges with Basil

Prep and cook time: About 30 minutes, plus at least 30 minutes to chill

1 Bring 1½ cups water and the sugar to a boil. Cook just until clear, 2 to 3 minutes. Let the syrup cool very briefly, then add the basil leaves. Set aside to steep and cool.

2 Rinse and hull the strawberries and cut them into quarters or sixths if they're very large. With a small, sharp knife, cut the ends off the oranges. Set 1 orange, cut side down, on a cutting board. Following its curve with the knife, slice off the peel and white pith. Holding the orange over a bowl to catch the juice, cut between the inner membranes and the fruit to release the segments into the bowl. Squeeze the juice from the membranes into the bowl and discard the membranes. Repeat with the remaining oranges. Add the strawberries to the oranges and pour the basil syrup over the fruit. Refrigerate at least 30 minutes before serving.

Makes 8 servings

³/4 **cup sugar**

¹/4 **cup thinly sliced fresh basil leaves**

4 **cups strawberries**

4 **navel oranges**

....

Notes from The Sunset Grill
You can make this salad several hours in advance, but don't store it too long or the berries will soften and lose their bright flavor.

Strawberries
Although fresh strawberries are increasingly available year-round, it's worth waiting for the unparalleled flavor of strawberries in season—from April to June. Choose bright red, small strawberries that look plump and juicy, and avoid any with soft patches. Wash and trim them just before using.

Fruit Wands with Vanilla-Rum Syrup and Pine Nut Panecillos

Prep and cook time: About 1¹/₂ hours

1. Prepare the Pine Nut Panecillos: Preheat the oven to 375°F. In a large frying pan over medium heat, stir or shake the pine nuts until lightly toasted, 3 minutes. Remove from the heat and let cool. In a food processor, process 1 cup of the pine nuts until smooth, scraping down the sides frequently. Add the butter, brown sugar, ¹/₂ cup granulated sugar, egg, and vanilla, then process to blend. In a separate bowl, stir together the flour and baking soda, then stir into the butter mixture until incorporated.

2. Brush two 9-inch cake pans with removable sides with butter. Divide the dough and press into the pans. Scatter the remaining pine nuts over the dough and press them lightly but firmly into it. Bake until the cookies begin to pull away from the sides of the pans and the centers spring back when lightly pressed, about 15 minutes. Meanwhile, in a small bowl, mix the remaining 4 teaspoons granulated sugar with the cinnamon. About 5 minutes before the cookies are done baking, sprinkle with the sugar-cinnamon mixture. Let the cookies cool in the pans about 10 minutes, then remove the rims. Cut each into 8 wedges and set aside until ready to serve.

3. While the Panecillos are baking, prepare the fruit wands: Put the sugar in a 2-quart pan. Using a small knife, slit the vanilla bean lengthwise. Scrape the seeds from the pod into the sugar, then add the pod. Stir in the rum, orange zest, and 2 cups water. Stir often over high heat until reduced to 1³/₄ cups, about 12 minutes. Remove the vanilla pod and let the syrup cool to room temperature. Meanwhile, trim and discard the ends from the star fruit. Cut the fruit crosswise into ¹/₂-inch slices. Slide a single piece of fruit onto each skewer if the skewers are very small, or 2 or 3 pieces of different fruits onto a single skewer if the skewers are larger.

4. Put the skewers, fruit end down, in a deep glass serving bowl. Pour the syrup over the fruit and serve the Panecillos alongside.

Makes 8 servings

1 cup sugar

1 vanilla bean (about 7 inches) or
    2 teaspoons vanilla

¹/₄ cup rum

2 tablespoons orange zest (long, thin
    shreds)

2 star fruit (about 6 ounces total),
    rinsed

2 cups fresh pineapple chunks

1 cup strawberries, hulled (optional)
    and rinsed

PINE NUT PANECILLOS

1¹/₄ cups pine nuts

¹/₂ cup unsalted butter, at room
    temperature, plus more for pans

¹/₂ cup firmly packed brown sugar

¹/₂ cup plus 4 teaspoons granulated
    sugar

1 egg

1 teaspoon vanilla

1³/₄ cups all-purpose flour

¹/₂ teaspoon baking soda

1 teaspoon ground cinnamon

Grilled Peaches with Vanilla Ice Cream

Prep and cook time: About 45 minutes

1 Prepare a grill for cooking over indirect heat. First, oil the grill rack. If using a charcoal grill, light 50 to 60 briquets and let burn until covered with ash, 20 to 30 minutes, then mound them to one side. Place a drip pan on the side cleared of coals. If using a gas grill, turn all burners to high and close the lid. When the grill is hot, lift the lid and turn off one of the burners. Place a drip pan under the turned-off burner—this is the indirect-heat area. Set the oiled grill rack in place.

2 In a small bowl, combine the brown sugar and the cinnamon. Cut the peaches along the seam all the way around and twist the halves off the pit. Brush the cut sides with the oil.

3 Lay the peaches, cut side down, on the grill rack over direct heat until the fruit has grill marks, 3 to 4 minutes. Brush the tops with oil, turn over, and move to the area cleared of coals. Sprinkle the cut sides with cinnamon sugar. Cover the grill (open vents for charcoal) and cook until the sugar is melted and fruit is tender, 10 to 15 minutes. Serve with vanilla ice cream and sprinkle on extra cinnamon sugar if you like.

Makes 4 servings

2 tablespoons light brown sugar

1/2 teaspoon cinnamon

4 fresh peaches

Grapeseed or olive oil

Vanilla ice cream

Peaches

Fresh ripe peaches, in season from June through August depending on the variety, are one of summer's best treats. For grilling, choose unbruised, firm-ripe fruits. You can check for ripeness with your nose: good-tasting peaches will have a strong, heady, sweet peach aroma.

Two Sherbets and a Sorbet

Prep and cook time for each: About 40 minutes, plus at least 6 hours to chill and freeze

For the Jasmine-Honey Sherbet: In a large bowl, whisk together all of the ingredients. Cover and chill until cold, at least 3 hours or up to 1 day. Freeze in an ice cream maker (at least 1 1/2-quart capacity), according to manufacturer's instructions, until machine stops or dasher is hard to turn. Transfer the sherbet to an airtight container and freeze until firm, about 3 hours.

For the Chocolate-Chai Sherbet: In a 3- to 4-quart pan over high heat, stir the chai tea and sugar until boiling. Remove from the heat. Whisk in the chocolate, cover, and let stand 10 minutes. Uncover and whisk to combine. Whisk in the half-and-half and the cinnamon, cardamom, and cloves. Cover and chill until cold, at least 3 hours or up to 1 day. Freeze in an ice cream maker (at least 1 1/2-quart capacity), according to the manufacturer's instructions, until machine stops or dasher is hard to turn. Transfer the sherbet to an airtight container and freeze until firm, about 3 hours.

For the Blackberry–Black Tea Sorbet: In a blender, purée the black-berries. Pour through a fine strainer into a bowl, pressing the pulp with a spatula to extract as much juice as possible (you should have about 2 cups purée). Discard solids. Whisk the tea and sugar into the purée. Cover and chill until cold, at least 3 hours or up to 1 day. Freeze in an ice cream maker (at least 1 1/2-quart capacity), according to manufacturer's instructions, until machine stops or dasher is hard to turn. Transfer the sorbet to an airtight container and freeze until firm, about 3 hours.

Makes about 6 servings

JASMINE-HONEY SHERBET

3 1/2 cups warm brewed green jasmine tea

3/4 cup half-and-half

3/4 cup honey

1/4 cup sugar

1/8 teaspoon fresh lemon juice

CHOCOLATE-CHAI SHERBET

3 1/2 cups chai tea

1/4 cup sugar

8 ounces chopped bittersweet chocolate

3/4 cup half-and-half

1/4 teaspoon ground cinnamon

1/4 teaspoon ground cardamom

1/4 teaspoon ground cloves

BLACKBERRY–BLACK TEA SORBET

1 1/2 pounds rinsed blackberries

2 cups brewed black Darjeeling or Assam tea

1 1/4 cups sugar

Triple-Decker Citrus Popsicles

Prep time: About 30 minutes, plus about 4¼ hours to freeze

1 Taste the blood orange juice. Add 1 tablespoon sugar and 1 teaspoon lemon juice and stir until sugar is completely dissolved. Taste again to see if it has the right sweetness and tartness for you, bearing in mind that when frozen, the juice will taste more subdued. Adjust the flavor by adding more sugar or lemon juice. Repeat with the tangerine and grapefruit juices, using the same range of sugar and lemon juice for each.

2 Fill each of 8 popsicle molds (see Notes) ⅓ of the way full with the blood orange juice and freeze, keeping them level and upright, until firm to the touch, about 45 minutes.

3 Fill each mold another ⅓ of the way full with the tangerine juice and freeze just until firm to the touch, another 45 minutes. Carefully insert the sticks, leaving 1½ to 2 inches sticking out. Freeze until the sticks feel solidly anchored, about 45 minutes.

4 Fill each mold to the top with the grapefruit juice, cover, and freeze 2 hours or overnight. To unmold the popsicles, run warm water over the individual molds just until they release from the sides, 5 to 15 seconds. Serve immediately.

Makes 8 popsicles

....

Notes from The Sunset Grill

The tastier the fruit you use, in any combination, the more delicious these bright, intense popsicles will be. You will need eight ⅓- to ½-cup popsicle molds, which are available at most cookware and hardware stores. Superfine sugar, available at most supermarkets, dissolves more quickly and thoroughly than regular sugar. If you can't find it, you can make your own by puréeing granulated sugar in a blender.

1 cup freshly squeezed blood orange juice (from 2 or 3 blood oranges)

About ¼ to ½ cup superfine sugar (see Notes)

1 to 2 tablespoons fresh lemon juice

1 cup freshly squeezed tangerine juice (from 3 or 4 large tangerines)

1 cup freshly squeezed white grapefruit juice (from 1 or 2 grapefruit)

Cherry and Chocolate Brownie Sundaes

Prep and cook time: About 1¹/₂ hours, plus 2¹/₂ hours to cool

1 Toss the fresh cherries with 1 tablespoon of the sugar and set aside.

2 Preheat the oven to 350°F. Butter a 9- by 13-inch pan. In a medium saucepan over very low heat, stir 1 cup butter and the chocolate, until just melted. Remove the mixture from the heat and let it cool slightly, about 5 minutes.

3 In a large bowl, whisk together the eggs, 2 cups sugar, vanilla, and salt. Slowly pour the chocolate-butter mixture into the egg mixture, whisking constantly. With a rubber spatula, gently fold in the flour. Add the dried cherries and chocolate chips and stir just until combined.

4 Spread the batter evenly into the baking pan and bake until the brownies are firm, beginning to pull away from the sides of the pan, and a toothpick inserted near the middle of the pan comes out nearly clean, about 35 minutes. Set the brownies on a cooling rack and let them cool completely. Meanwhile, make the Dark Chocolate Sauce.

5 Cut half of the pan of brownies into 1-inch chunks. Divide the brownie chunks evenly among 8 to 10 sundae dishes or shallow bowls. Top the chunks with a generous scoop of ice cream, some of the Dark Chocolate Sauce, and the fresh cherries. Serve immediately.

Makes 8 to 10 servings

....

Notes from The Sunset Grill

Save the leftover brownies for eating out of hand with a tall glass of milk. The recipe for Dark Chocolate Sauce makes about 2 cups. Any leftover sauce can be kept, covered, in the refrigerator up to 2 weeks. Warm the sauce before serving.

1 pound fresh Bing cherries, pitted and quartered

2 cups plus 1 tablespoon sugar

1 cup unsalted butter, plus more for pan

8 ounces good-quality bittersweet chocolate, broken into large chunks

5 eggs

1 tablespoon vanilla

¹/₄ teaspoon salt

1¹/₃ cups all-purpose flour

²/₃ cup dried Bing cherries

1 cup dark chocolate or semisweet chocolate chips

1 gallon cherry ice cream

Dark Chocolate Sauce (see page 241)

Nectarine-Boysenberry Crisp

Prep and cook time: About 1 hour

1 Preheat the oven to 350°F. Rinse the nectarines and berries. Cut the nectarines off their pits into 1/2-inch-thick wedges and drop into a large bowl. Add the berries, granulated sugar, and lemon juice, and mix gently just until combined.

2 In another bowl, stir the brown sugar, flour, rolled oats, vanilla, cinnamon, nutmeg, and salt until well combined. Add the butter and cut it in with a pastry blender or rub it in with your fingers until the mixture resembles coarse meal. Stir in the pecans.

3 Spread the fruit mixture level in a shallow 2- to 2 1/2-quart baking dish. Sprinkle the oat-pecan mixture over the top.

4 Bake until the juices at the edges of the baking dish are bubbling and the top is crisp and golden, 40 to 45 minutes.

Makes 8 to 10 servings

....

Notes from The Sunset Grill

This crisp tastes best warm, but you can also serve it at room temperature.

1 1/2 **pounds firm-ripe nectarines**

2 **cups boysenberries or blackberries**

1/4 **cup granulated sugar**

2 **tablespoons fresh lemon juice**

3/4 **cup firmly packed brown sugar**

2/3 **cup all-purpose flour**

1/2 **cup rolled oats**

1 **teaspoon vanilla**

1 **teaspoon ground cinnamon**

1/4 **teaspoon ground nutmeg**

1/4 **teaspoon salt**

1/2 **cup cold unsalted butter, cut into** 1/2-**inch pieces**

3/4 **cup pecans, chopped**

Fresh Apricot Crisp

Prep and cook time: About 1 hour, plus about 30 minutes to cool

1   Preheat the oven to 350°F and butter an 8- by 8-inch baking pan. Melt 1/2 cup butter and let cool. Whisk together the flour, cinnamon, ginger, nutmeg, cloves, salt, and brown sugar. Stir in the rolled oats, raisins, and almonds, then stir in the melted butter.

2   Toss the apricots with the lemon juice and granulated sugar and spread in the baking pan. Squeeze the topping into shaggy chunks and scatter over the apricots. Bake until the juices at the edges of the baking dish are bubbling and the top is crisp and golden, about 40 minutes. Serve with vanilla ice cream if you like.

Makes 8 servings

....

Notes from The Sunset Grill

If you can find Blenheim apricots, use them. If you are using most other varieties, cut each into quarters, increase the lemon juice to 2 tablespoons and the granulated sugar to 1/2 cup, and mix a pinch each of cinnamon, ginger, and nutmeg into the fruit before baking.

1/2 **cup unsalted butter, plus more for pan**

1/2 **cup all-purpose flour**

1/2 **teaspoon ground cinnamon**

1/2 **teaspoon ginger**

1/2 **teaspoon nutmeg**

1/4 **teaspoon ground cloves**

1/4 **teaspoon salt**

1/3 **cup firmly packed dark brown sugar**

2/3 **cup quick-cooking rolled oats**

1/3 **cup golden raisins**

1/3 **cup chopped almonds**

5 **cups (about 15) fresh apricots, pitted and halved (see Notes)**

1 **tablespoon fresh lemon juice**

1/4 **cup granulated sugar**

Ginger-Chocolate Cookies

Prep and cook time: About 1 hour

1   Preheat the oven to 350°F. Butter a large baking sheet and set aside. In a medium bowl, whisk the flour, cocoa powder, ginger, baking soda, cinnamon, nutmeg, and salt until thoroughly combined. Set aside.

2   In a large bowl, beat the 3/4 cup butter and the brown sugar until light and fluffy, about 3 minutes. Add the molasses, egg, and vanilla, and beat to combine.

3   Mix in the dry ingredients gently but thoroughly, scraping down the sides of the bowl as necessary. The batter will be thick. Stir in the chopped chocolate until well combined.

4   Take about 2 tablespoons of the batter and shape it into a ball. Repeat with the remaining batter. (If the batter is too sticky, dampen the palms of your hands with water when rolling the balls.) Roll the balls in the granulated sugar, and place 12 balls on the buttered baking sheet. Dip the bottom of a glass in water and use it to flatten the balls to a thickness of about 1/4 inch, rewetting the glass as necessary to prevent the batter from sticking.

5   Bake the cookies, one baking sheet at a time, until just set, about 10 minutes. Cool the cookies in the pan for 5 minutes, then transfer to cooling racks to cool completely.

Makes about 36 cookies

....

Notes from The Sunset Grill
The cookies will keep up to 2 days in an airtight container at room temperature.

3/4 cup unsalted butter, plus more for baking sheet

2 cups all-purpose flour

1/3 cup unsweetened cocoa powder

2 1/2 tablespoons ground ginger

2 teaspoons baking soda

1 1/2 teaspoons cinnamon

1 1/2 teaspoons freshly ground nutmeg

1/2 teaspoon salt

1 cup firmly packed light brown sugar

1/4 cup molasses

1 egg

1 teaspoon vanilla extract

8 ounces bittersweet chocolate, finely chopped

1/3 cup granulated sugar

Lemon-Basil Shortbread

Prep and cook time: About 1 hour, plus about 30 minutes to cool

1 Preheat the oven to 300°F. In a food processor, mix the butter, 1/2 cup sugar, lemon zest, lemon juice, flour, cornstarch, and basil leaves until smooth. Press the dough into two 8-inch cake pans with removable sides. Press the tines of a fork around the edge of the dough, then pierce the dough with the fork in parallel lines about an inch apart.

2 Bake the shortbread until firm to the touch and slightly browned, about 45 minutes. While still hot, sprinkle each shortbread round with 1 tablespoon sugar. Remove the sides from the pans and cut each round, while still warm, into 12 wedges. Set the pans on cooling racks to cool completely, then remove the shortbread wedges and serve.

Makes 24 cookies

1 cup unsalted butter, at room temperature

1/2 cup plus 2 tablespoons sugar

1 teaspoon grated lemon zest

1 tablespoon fresh lemon juice

2 1/2 cups all-purpose flour

6 tablespoons cornstarch

1 tablespoon minced fresh basil leaves

Notes from The Sunset Grill

Shortbread cookies will keep up to 1 week in an airtight container at room temperature.

Basil
The quintessential summer herb, tender basil leaves add a refreshing, distinctive quality to desserts as well as to savory dishes. Their slightly spicy herbal character pairs particularly well with lemon's tartness. Look for fresh, glossy, bright green bunches of basil with tender stems, and mince the leaves just before using to maintain its fresh color.

Chocolate-Almond Torte

Prep and cook time: About 1 hour, plus about 30 minutes to cool

1 Preheat the oven to 350°F. Butter and flour a 9-inch cake pan. In a food processor, pulse the almonds until finely ground.

2 In a large bowl of a mixer set on medium-high speed, beat the butter and 1/2 cup of the sugar until light and fluffy. Add the egg yolks, one at a time, beating well after each addition. Add the chocolate, vanilla, and almonds, and beat thoroughly. Gently fold in the buckwheat flour.

3 In a medium bowl of a mixer set on medium-high speed, whisk the egg whites until foamy. Add the salt and whisk until soft, glossy peaks form. Whisk in the remaining 1/4 cup sugar. Gently fold 1/4 of the beaten egg whites into the chocolate mixture, and then fold in the remaining whites. Pour the cake batter into the pan.

4 Bake until a knife inserted in the center of the cake comes out clean, about 30 minutes. Set the cake on a cooling rack and let cool for 10 minutes. Slide a knife between the cake and the side of the pan, then invert the cake onto a plate and let it cool completely. Dust with powdered sugar and serve.

Makes 10 servings

6 tablespoons unsalted butter,
plus more for pan

1 1/2 cups sliced almonds

3/4 cup sugar

4 eggs, separated

6 ounces semisweet chocolate,
melted and cooled

2 teaspoons vanilla extract

1/2 cup buckwheat flour

1/4 teaspoon salt

Powdered sugar

Almonds
Ground almonds add flavor, a subtle nubbly texture, and crucial structure to cakes like this one that contain no wheat flour. Grinding them is easy—just be sure to pulse briefly so they don't turn to nut butter. If time is short, you can use packaged fine almond meal.

Chocolate-Chip Shortcakes with Berries and Dark Chocolate Sauce

Prep and cook time: About 1 hour

1 Preheat the oven to 375°F. In the bowl of a food processor, combine 3 cups flour, 3 tablespoons of the sugar, the baking powder, and salt, and process until blended. Add 1/2 cup cold butter and pulse until fine crumbs form. Add 1 cup of the heavy cream and pulse just until the dough comes together.

2 Turn the dough onto a lightly floured work surface and press to flatten it slightly. Sprinkle the chocolate chips over the dough, then knead until incorporated, 6 to 8 turns. Pat the dough into a round about 1 1/4 inches thick. With a 2 3/4-inch round cutter, cut out rounds from the dough. Gather the dough and pat out again as needed to cut out 6 rounds, dusting the work surface with more flour to prevent sticking. Set the rounds on a baking sheet, brush the tops with the melted butter, and sprinkle generously with sugar.

3 Bake the shortcakes until golden brown, 20 to 25 minutes. Let them cool on a cooling rack at least 15 minutes. Meanwhile, prepare the berries, chocolate sauce, and whipped cream. For the berries: In a bowl, gently mix the remaining 3 tablespoons sugar, the berries, and the mint. Set aside. For the Dark Chocolate Sauce: In a medium saucepan over low heat, stir the heavy cream and chocolate until smooth, about 15 minutes. Stir in the vanilla, remove from the heat, and keep warm. For the whipped cream: In a large bowl with a mixer set on medium-high speed, beat the remaining 1 cup heavy cream until soft peaks form.

4 With a serrated knife, slice the shortcakes in half horizontally. Set the bottom halves on plates and top with the berry mixture, Dark Chocolate Sauce, and some whipped cream. Set the tops in place and serve immediately.

Makes 6 servings

About 3 cups all-purpose flour

6 tablespoons sugar, plus some for sprinkling

1 1/2 tablespoons baking powder

1/2 teaspoon salt

1/2 cup cold unsalted butter, cut into chunks, plus about 1 tablespoon melted

2 cups heavy cream

3/4 cup mini dark chocolate or semisweet chocolate chips

4 cups blackberries, raspberries, or a combination of the two

1/4 cup finely chopped fresh mint leaves

DARK CHOCOLATE SAUCE

1 cup heavy cream

6 ounces dark (bittersweet) chocolate, chopped

1 teaspoon vanilla

Notes from The Sunset Grill
The recipe for Dark Chocolate Sauce makes about 2 cups. Any left-over sauce can be kept, covered, in the refrigerator up to 2 weeks.

Brambleberry Pie

Prep and cook time: 2 hours, plus about 45 minutes to chill dough and 3 hours to cool

1 Prepare the Pie Pastry: Mix the flour, sugar, and salt in a large bowl. Drop in the butter and shortening. Using a fork, work the butter and shortening into the flour mixture until it resembles cornmeal with some small pea-size pieces. With the fork, quickly stir in 1/2 cup ice water (the mixture will not hold together). Turn the dough and crumbs onto a clean work surface. Knead just until the dough starts to hold together, 5 to 10 turns. Divide the dough in half and pat each half into a 6-inch disk. Wrap each disk in plastic wrap and refrigerate until firm, at least 30 minutes.

2 Set an oven rack in the bottom third of the oven and preheat to 375°F. Lightly dust the work surface and a rolling pin with flour, then unwrap one disk of dough. Roll the dough into a 12-inch round, turning 90° after every 3 or 4 passes of the rolling pin. Transfer the dough to a 9-inch pie pan. Trim the dough so only 1/4 inch is left hanging over the rim. Cover the pie shell with plastic wrap and refrigerate until firm, at least 15 minutes. Meanwhile, roll the second disk into an 11-inch round. Transfer the round to a baking sheet, cover with plastic wrap, and refrigerate until firm.

3 Meanwhile, prepare the filling: Put the berries in a large bowl. Sprinkle with 1/4 cup flour, 1/4 cup granulated sugar, the brown sugar, tapioca, lemon juice, and salt. Stir gently until the berries are well coated. Taste and add more granulated sugar if you like. Pour the berry mixture into the chilled bottom crust and dot with the butter. Unwrap the top crust and lay it over the pie. Fold the bottom crust edge up over the edge of the top crust and crimp the edges together. Cut several vents in the top crust and sprinkle with the remaining 1 teaspoon granulated sugar. Put the pie on a rimmed baking sheet and bake until the crust is browned and the filling is bubbling, about 1 hour and 10 minutes.

4 Let the pie cool on a cooling rack until the bottom of the pie pan reaches room temperature, at least 3 hours. Serve with whipped cream or vanilla ice cream if you like.

Makes 8 servings

5 cups raspberries, blackberries, marion-berries, or other brambleberries

About 1/4 cup all-purpose flour

About 1/4 cup plus 1 teaspoon granulated sugar

1/4 cup firmly packed light brown sugar

1 tablespoon quick-cooking tapioca

1 tablespoon fresh lemon juice

1 teaspoon salt

1 tablespoon unsalted butter

Whipped cream or vanilla ice cream (optional)

PIE PASTRY

2 1/2 cups all-purpose flour

1 tablespoon sugar

1 1/2 teaspoons salt

7 tablespoons very cold unsalted butter, cut into small pieces

7 tablespoons very cold shortening, cut into pieces

Triple Coconut Cream Mini Pies

Prep and cook time: About 1¹/2 hours, plus at least 3 hours to chill

1 Make the Coconut Pastry Cream: In a saucepan over medium-high heat, simmer the milk, sweetened coconut, and the seeds and pod of the vanilla bean (see page 221). In a bowl, whisk together the eggs, sugar, and flour. While whisking, slowly pour about 1/3 of the hot milk mixture into the egg mixture, then slowly whisk the egg-milk mixture back into the saucepan. Whisk over medium-high heat until the pastry cream thickens and bubbles, 5 minutes. Remove from the heat, discard the vanilla bean, and stir in the butter. Spoon the hot pastry cream into a bowl and set in a larger bowl of ice water, stirring occasionally, until cool. Press plastic wrap directly onto the surface of the pastry cream and chill until cold, at least 3 hours.

2 Meanwhile, prepare the Coconut Pie Shells: In a food processor, pulse the flour, sweetened coconut, butter, sugar, and salt to form coarse crumbs. Add 4 tablespoons ice water, 1 tablespoon at a time, pulsing after each addition. Divide into 9 equal pieces, forming each into a small disk, wrap with plastic wrap, and chill at least 30 minutes. Lightly dust the work surface and a rolling pin with flour. Unwrap the disks and set on the work surface. Roll each disk into a 5-inch round. Transfer the rounds to nine 3¹/2-inch fluted nonstick brioche molds. Trim any dough that overhangs the molds flush with the rims. Prick the bottoms with a fork and chill for 1 hour. Set an oven rack in the bottom third of the oven and preheat to 400°F. Lay a small piece of parchment paper in each shell and fill it with dried beans. Put the shells on a cookie sheet and bake until golden brown, 10 minutes. Remove the beans and parchment and continue baking the shells until the bottoms are dark golden brown, about 10 minutes more. Let the shells cool completely.

3 To fill the pies, remove the shells from the molds. Spoon in the pastry cream, filling each shell a little more than halfway. Whip the cream with the 1/3 cup sugar and the vanilla until stiff peaks form. Fill a pastry bag fitted with a large star tip (no. 6) with the whipped cream and pipe it into each shell, or simply spoon it on. With a vegetable peeler, scrape wide curls from the white chocolate over the cream, top with the toasted coconut, and serve.

Makes 9 mini pies

2¹/2 cups heavy cream

¹/3 cup sugar

1 teaspoon vanilla

1 3-ounce chunk white chocolate, at room temperature

1 cup unsweetened "chip" coconut or ¹/2 cup unsweetened shredded coconut, toasted in a 350°F oven until golden, about 10 minutes

COCONUT PASTRY CREAM

2 cups milk

2 cups sweetened shredded coconut

1 vanilla bean, split in half lengthwise

2 eggs

¹/2 cup plus 2 tablespoons sugar

3 tablespoons all-purpose flour

4 tablespoons unsalted butter, softened

COCONUT PIE SHELLS

1 cup plus 2 tablespoons all-purpose flour, plus more for work surface

¹/2 cup sweetened shredded coconut

¹/2 cup cold unsalted butter, cut into ¹/2-inch cubes

2 teaspoons sugar

¹/4 teaspoon coarse kosher salt

Mango-Mint Agua Fresca

3 pounds firm-ripe mangoes

4 cups fresh orange juice

1/2 cup lightly packed fresh mint leaves, plus
    several sprigs, rinsed and drained

About 1/4 cup fresh lemon juice

Cut and discard the pits and peel from the mangoes,
then cut fruit into chunks. In a blender or food processor, in batches, pulse the mangoes, orange juice,
mint leaves, and 5 cups water until smoothly puréed.
Pour the mixture into a pitcher. Stir in 1/4 cup lemon
juice, or more to taste. Pour the mixture into ice-
filled glasses, garnish with mint sprigs, and serve.

Makes 8 servings

Pomegranate-Orange Cooler

5 cups fresh pomegranate juice

2 1/2 cups vodka

1/3 cup orange-flavored liqueur

1/3 cup fresh lime juice

2 1/2 cups chilled ginger ale

Orange slices (optional)

In a pitcher, combine the pomegranate juice, vodka,
orange-flavored liqueur, and lime juice. Cover and
chill until very cold, at least 1 hour. Just before
serving, stir in the ginger ale. Pour the mixture into
ice-filled glasses, garnish with the orange slices if
you like, and serve.

Makes 8 to 10 servings

....

Notes from The Sunset Grill

*For a nonalcoholic version of the drink, omit the
vodka, replace the liqueur with fresh orange juice,
and increase the ginger ale to 5 cups.*

Lemon Grass and Ginger Iced Tea

1 stalk fresh lemon grass

1/2 cup sugar

7 thin slices fresh ginger

5 bags green tea

Rinse the lemon grass, cut into 2-inch lengths, and
crush with the flat side of a large knife. In a 2-quart
pan, bring 5 cups water and the sugar, ginger, and
lemon grass to a boil. Take off the heat and add the
green-tea bags. Let the tea steep about 4 minutes
or until the flavor is as strong as you like. Discard
the tea bags and let the tea cool, about 30 minutes.
Pour the tea through a fine strainer into a pitcher,
then cover and chill until cold, at least 2 hours. Serve
the tea in tall glasses, over ice cubes if you like.

Makes 4 servings

Basil Lemonade

1/2 cup lightly packed fresh basil leaves, plus
    a few sprigs, rinsed and drained

About 3 tablespoons sugar

1/2 cup fresh lemon juice

In a 1 1/2- to 2-quart glass measure or bowl, combine
the basil leaves and 3 tablespoons sugar. With a
wooden spoon, crush the sugar and the leaves until
thoroughly bruised. Add 4 cups water and the lemon
juice. Stir the mixture until the sugar is dissolved,
1 to 2 minutes. Taste the lemonade and add more
sugar if necessary. Pour the lemonade through a fine
strainer into ice-filled glasses, garnish with sprigs of
fresh basil, and serve.

Makes 4 servings

....

Notes from The Sunset Grill

*All basils add fragrance to lemonade, but colored
varieties contribute extra personality. Dark purple
basils tint the lemonade pink but have a milder flavor
than green varieties. Choose your favorite.*

Mojito

40 fresh mint leaves, plus mint sprigs for garnish, rinsed and drained

4 teaspoons superfine sugar

About 1/2 cup light rum

6 tablespoons fresh lime juice

About 1/2 cup chilled soda water

Divide the mint leaves between two 8- to 10-ounce glasses, then add 2 teaspoons of the superfine sugar to each glass. With the handle of a wooden spoon, coarsely crush the mint leaves and the sugar. Divide the light rum and the lime juice between the glasses, then top each with a few ice cubes and the chilled soda water. Garnish with the sprigs of mint and serve.

Makes 2 servings

Peach Martini

2 ripe white peaches, thinly sliced

1 fresh chile, such as red or green jalapeño or Thai chile, cut into 6 slices

Kosher salt

1/8 to 1/4 cup dry vermouth

1 1/2 cups gin or vodka

Chill 6 martini glasses, empty, in the freezer. Meanwhile, for each drink, push a few slices of peach and 1 slice of chile onto a small wooden skewer or toothpick. Lightly season the peaches and chile with the kosher salt. Pour 1 to 2 teaspoons dry vermouth into each chilled glass. Swirl the glasses to coat with the vermouth, then pour out the vermouth. Fill a 3-cup martini shaker with ice cubes and the gin or vodka. Seal the shaker and shake until cold, 4 to 6 shakes. Strain the gin or vodka into the glasses, garnish each with a peach-chile skewer, and serve.

Makes 6 servings

Lime Rickey

1/2 cup sugar

1 1/2 cups gin

3/4 cup fresh lime juice

1 1/2 quarts chilled soda water

Thin slices of lime

In a 1-quart pan over low heat, stir the sugar with 1/2 cup water until the sugar is dissolved, about 5 minutes. Let the sugar syrup cool. In a 3-quart pitcher, combine the gin, lime juice, and cooled syrup. Cover and freeze the mixture until very cold, at least 20 minutes. To serve, add the soda water, pour into ice-filled glasses, and garnish with the slices of lime.

Makes 6 to 8 servings

Pimm's Cup

2 oranges, halved and cut into slices

2 lemons, halved and cut into slices

1 Persian cucumber or one 3-inch length of English cucumber, washed and sliced

2 cups Pimm's No. 1

4 cups lemon-lime soda

6 to 8 large sprigs mint, crushed gently, plus several loose leaves, rinsed and drained

Fill two 5-cup pitchers 1/4 full with ice cubes. Top each with a layer of orange slices, a few lemon slices, and a layer of cucumber slices. Repeat with the remaining orange, lemon, and cucumber slices. Pour in the Pimm's and the soda, dividing them equally between the pitchers. Mix the contents of each pitcher with a long-handled wooden spoon. With the spoon, push the mint sprigs and leaves down into the pitchers. Divide the mixture among 8 tall glasses, with a few slices of fruit and cucumber and a few mint leaves in each glass.

Makes 8 servings

index

Sunset

Vice President, Editorial Director: Bob Doyle

Director of Sales: Brad Moses

Director of Operations: Rosann Sutherland

Marketing Manager: Linda Barker

Art Director: Vasken Guiragossian

Editor: Val Cipollone

Designer: Catherine Jacobes

Senior editor: Ben Marks

Contributing writers: Jean Galton and
    Kate Washington

Copyeditor and proofreader: Denise Griffiths

Indexer: Ken DellaPenta

Food stylist: George Dolese

Assistant food stylist: Elisabet Nederlanden

Prepress coordinator: Eligio Hernández

Production specialist: Linda M. Bouchard

First edition.
First Printing, March 2008.
10 9 8 7 6 5 4 3 2 1

ISBN-13: 978-0-376-02722-1
ISBN-10: 0-376-02722-3
Library of Congress Control Number: 2007940185

Printed in the United States of America.

For additional copies of *The Sunset Grill* or any other Sunset book, visit us at www.sunsetbooks.com.

For more grilling recipes, visit
myrecipes.com

ACKNOWLEDGMENTS

Numerous writers and editors at *Sunset* contributed to the recipes in this book. The dedication to perfection on the part of the *Sunset* staff, whether it's from behind a grill or behind a computer, is what makes all *Sunset* recipes so enduring and trustworthy. In particular, we'd like to thank the magazine's Food Editor, Margo True, for her early and enthusiastic encouragement; Executive Editor Dale Conour for helping us choose many of the recipes; and Editor-in-Chief Katie Tamony, for sharing *Sunset*'s recipes and photography with us so that we could share them with you.

PHOTOGRAPHY CREDITS

Unless otherwise credited, all photographs are by Noel Barnhurst.

T = top, B = bottom, L = left, R = right, M = middle

Leigh Beisch: CoverBL, 13BL, 29, 30, 34, 41, 174, 220, 247TL; Annabelle Breakey: 42, 49, 173, 177, 244; Rob D. Brodman: 10TL, 218BL; James Carrier: CoverTL, CoverBR, 1, 8L, 10BR, 11BL, 13TL, 14BL, 14BR, 15TL, 59BL, 93, 97, 127TL, 127TR, 162, 178, 197, 198, 210, 247BR; James Carriére: 53; Corbis/JupiterImages.com: 238BL; Sheri Giblin/Jupiter Images.com: CoverTM, 33; Dan Goldberg: 46, 47BL, 110, 231, 236; Andrea Gomez: 51BL; Leo Gong: 45, 50, 58, 61, 62, 65, 145, 228; Thayer Allyson Gowdy: 9, 75BR, 235; Art Gray: 70; ©istockphoto.com: 44BL, 124BL, 192BL; Jupiter Images/Brand X Pictures: 67BL; Dave Lauridsen: 222BL; Valerie Martin: 69; Ericka McConnell: 4TR, 4BL, 248TR; Ngoc Minh Ngo: 11TL; Victoria Pearson: 227; Linda Lamb Peters: 63BL; Scott Peterson: 224; Norm Plate: 14TL, 14TR, 15TR; David Prince: 243; Lisa Romerein: CoverTR, 2, 5TL, 13BR, 15BL, 48BL, 75TL, 75TR, 142, 149TL, 216, 240, 247BL, 248BL, 248BR; Christina Schmidhofer: 5BL; Karen Steffens: 31BL; Thomas J. Story: 10TR, 12BL, 19, 26, 32BL, 102, 114, 134, 219, 232, 237BL, 248TL; Lance Walheim: 128BL; Barry Wong/GettyImages.com: 188BL; Westend 61-WEP/GettyImages.com: 196BL.